Principles of Socialism

Manifesto of Nineteenth Century Democracy

Washington Studies in World Intellectual History
Executive Editor
Robert Merrill

A book series on the relationship between formal systems of thought and the social and political contexts those systems interpret. Our books study the structure and dynamics of intellect communities and their impact on the lives of everyday people.

Manuscripts and proposals for this series are invited. Please contact the editor: Maisonneuve Press, P.O. Box 2980, Washington, DC 20013 or rm@maisonneuvepress.com

Vol. 1. *Church Clothes: Land, Mission, and the End of Apartheid in South Africa*, Thomas Patrick Wilkinson (2004).

Vol. 2. *Principles of Socialism: Manifesto of Nineteenth Century Democracy*, Victor Consliderant. Translated by Joan Roelofs (2006)

PRINCIPLES OF SOCIALISM

MANIFESTO OF NINETEENTH CENTURY DEMOCRACY

Victor Considerant

Translated by Joan Roelofs

Washington Studies in World Intellectual History, Volume 2

Maisonneuve Press
Washington, D.C
2006

Victor Considerant
Principles of Socialism: Manifesto of 19th Century Democracy

Translated by Joan Roelofs

Washington Studies in World Intellectual History, Volume 2

© 2006 Maisonneuve Press
P.O. Box 2980
Washington, DC 20013-2980

http://www.maisonneuvepress.com

Maisonneuve Press is a division of the Institute for Advanced Cultural Studies, a non-profit collective of scholars concerned with the critical study of culture. Write to the Director for information about other Institute programs and activities of the Press.

Library of Congress Cataloging-in-Publication Data

Considerant, Victor, 1808-1893.
  [Principes du socialisme. English]
  Principles of socialism : manifesto of nineteenth century democracy / Victor Considerant ; translated by Joan Roelofs.
      p. cm. — (Washington studies in world intellectual history ; v. 2)
  Includes bibliographical references and index.
  ISBN 0-944624-47-2 (alk. paper)
  1. Communism—France. 2. Socialism—France. I. Title. II. Series.
  HX704.C7M53 2005
  335'.2—dc22
                                                    2005025424
  ISBN 10   0-944624-47-0
  ISBN 13   978-0-944624-47-0

Cover: Detail from Frédéric Sorrieu, *La République universelle démocratique et sociale - Le Pacte* (1848)

Table of Contents

Acknowledgements

This project evolved from my great admiration for the early 19th century socialist, Charles Fourier. As this is a rare mania among political scientists, I was sometimes called upon to perform essential scholarly services. Fourier's leading disciple was Victor Considerant; consequently, I was asked by *New Political Science* to review Jonathan Beecher's 2001 biography: *Victor Considerant and the Rise and Fall of French Romantic Socialism*. I had previously read Rondel V. Davidson's 1977 article: "Reform versus Revolution: Victor Considerant and the *Communist Manifesto*," comparing the two manifestos, and now learned that Considerant's had never been translated into English. When my retirement provided an opening, I decided to do it myself.

The ground had been prepared by my pleasure in translating from French, cultivated in LeRoy Breunig's course at Barnard College. In graduate school I was encouraged by Albert Somit, for whose course I translated selections from Henri-Claude de Saint-Simon's writings. For general support and/or help in finding historically appropriate English terms, I thank Diana Greene, Gretchen Muller, Bertell Ollman, Darko Suvin, and Victor Wallis. I was fortunate to discover a world conclave of freelance translators, who compete among themselves in providing answers to the perplexed. They can be found at the KudoZ page of www.ProZ.com.

Credit is also due to the long-dead compilers of *Spiers and Surenne's French and English Dictionary* [1852]. The Keene State College Library has a very helpful staff, and allows me access to the *Oxford English Dictionary* online. I received thorough, efficient, and gracious responses to an orthographical question (*i.e.*, there is no accent in Considerant) from Carol Armbruster, French Area Specialist, Library of Congress, and Jean-Louis Pailhès, Département de recherche bibliographique, Bibliothèque Nationale de France.

My publisher and editor, Robert Merrill, has provided a pleasant and collaborative process.

Finally, for inspiration, encouragement, information, and helpful critique, I am deeply grateful to Jonathan Beecher and Gareth Stedman Jones.

Translator's Introduction

Why is this document important?

First, as a matter of curiosity. There have been persistent rumors by scholars and activists that the 1848 *Communist Manifesto* of Marx and Engels was in large part plagiarized from Victor Considerant's *Principes du Socialisme: Manifeste de la démocratie au XIX siècle,* first published in 1843 as an introduction to his new journal, *La Démocratie pacifique*.[1] In 1847, it was reprinted in pamphlet form (henceforth referred to as *Manifeste*). There is evidence from their own diaries that both Marx and Engels were familiar with the *Manifeste*. On the other hand, Considerant probably never met Marx, and in 1843, had not even heard of him. Jonathan Beecher concluded:

> In the course of his own study Marx almost certainly read Considerant's *Manifeste politique et sociale de la démocratie pacifique* (published shortly before Marx's arrival in Paris), parts of *Destinée sociale*, and probably other works as well. In these readings Marx seems to have been particularly engaged by Considerant's critique of bourgeois society and the capitalist economy.[2]

Paris in the 1830s and 1840s was the locus of radical émigré activity and the seedbed of Marxism. There German philosophical concepts of alienation derived from G. W. F. Hegel and Ludwig Feuerbach were combined with the French socialist critics of "political economy," such as J. C. L. Simonde de Sismondi, Henri-Claude de Saint-Simon, and Charles Fourier. The latter, rejecting the "utopian" notions of Adam Smith and Jean Baptiste Say, maintained that the "free market" resulted in class conflict, anarchic competition, monopolization, overproduction, "new feudalism," and rule by property owners, regardless of political institutions. It is clear that the *Communist Manifesto* emerged from these roots, with some inspiration from the British Robert Owen.

Rondel V. Davidson has made an extensive comparison of the texts and found striking similarities in the critique of capitalism offered by both documents.[3] The great difference lies in their conclusions, for Considerant *warns* that revolution will occur if social reform is not instituted; he advocates peaceful social transformation, without revolutionary violence or the total abolition of private property.

Although brief excerpts of the Considerant *Manifeste* have been translated into English, there is no evidence of any previous English translation of the entire document.[4] Therefore, this publication will help readers to make their own judgments about plagiarism; the French text is available online for verification.[5]

The document is also inherently interesting, especially since scorned ideas are currently being re-evaluated. In France, disillusionment with Marxism and the revival of anarchism brought Charles Fourier's theories back onto the stage in 1968. Skepticism about the "revolutionary project" and indications of a shrinking proletariat have led to searches for a "third way," or at least, a different way.[6] Marxism was also challenged by the Green movement that arose in the 1970s, calling attention to feminist, ecological, and multicultural concerns neglected by traditional radical parties.

Post-modernism and post-Marxism disturbed the rigid categories and boxes into which ideas and ideologies have been stuffed by scholars and activists. "Utopian socialism" was a label that had stuck. It was used first by capitalists and then by Marx and Engels, loyal bedfellows in this conspiracy at least, to discredit early socialists. Today there are more people willing to admit that both "the invisible hand" of capitalism and the "proletarian revolution" of Marxism could fit into the "utopian" box, while the so-called "utopians" were brimming with practical suggestions and experimental, rational, and peaceful methods for healing society's woes.[7] Even their visionary, imaginative, and rather fantastic aspects had the very practical effect of serving as recruitment tools.

Similarly, distinctions between the terms "rationalist" and "romantic" need to be revisited. By the 1840s, both socialist and communist doctrines were a blend of many elements. The Fourierists, despite a "romantic" glorification of diversity, were also "rationalist" in their proposal for a minimum of civilized existence for all, the use of social science to attain the major social goal – human happiness, the testing of all institutions against that goal, and the overarching requirement of peace. Marxian Communism claimed to be the only *scientific* socialism, yet it appealed to heroic figures and especially the heroic class of proletarians to reach its rather vague goals. When specified, these goals generally led back to Fourierism, e. g.: ". . . an association in which the free development of each is the condition for the free development of all."[8] Similarly, the politically significant phenomenon of Freemasonry during this period expressed, on the one hand, fascination with science, and ideals of brotherhood, peace, and rational organization; on the other, occultism, ritual, and spectacle.

The two inspirations for this translation are related. Many prefer to see socialist camps as mutually hostile, cultish outcroppings, yet socialism has had considerable co-operative development, with shared ideas, slogans, and even plagiarized theoretical writings. The concept of plagiarism, closely related to the idea of private property, is currently undergoing revisionism, especially when applied to socialist doctrine. In addition, many of our heroes among artists, composers, writers, and scientists might be culpable if we applied today's standards of attribution to earlier cultural productions. Here is a situationist view:

> "The new revolutionary theory," the situationist Mustapha Khayati wrote in 1966, "cannot advance without redefining its fundamental concepts. 'Ideas improve,' says Lautremont. 'The meaning of words participates in the movement. Plagiarism is necessary. Progress implies it. It embraces an author's phrase, makes use of his or her expressions, erases a false idea, and replaces it with the right idea.' To salvage Marx's thought it is necessary continually to make it more precise, to correct it, to reformulate it in the light of a hundred years of reinforcement of alienation and the possibilities of negating it." The situationists, in their attempts to develop a coherent critique of society as it really is, plagiarized the writings of Marx, Hegel, Fourier, Lewis

Carroll, Sade, Lautremont, the surrealists, Henri Lefebvre, Georg Lukacs – in short, from anyone whose basic impulse was to theorize the totality of society. Yet, unlike nearly all of the theorists and artists from whom they plagiarized, the situationists critiqued society without the pull of allegiances or the fear of reprisals. The SI never pretended to have a monopoly on intelligence, but on its use.[9]

Accusations are plentiful among the socialists and their fore-bears, and they are not without merit. Pierre Leroux, a Saint-Simonian, claimed that Fourier plagiarized Diderot, Restif de la Bretonne, and Saint-Simon.[10] Engels pooh-poohs this latter charge. Flora Tristan, a feminist inspired by Fourier, argued that his work drew heavily on Francesco Doni's (1513-1574). Doni's uto-pian writings were produced after he served as the printer for the Italian translation of Thomas More's *Utopia*. Similarly, Proudhon, as a printer in Besançon, had close acquaintance with Fourier's work.

The readers of the present translation can decide whether the ideas or the phrases of the *Communist Manifesto* were plagiarized from Considerant. If so, does it matter, and from whom did Considerant plagiarize?

This issue opens up a long trail of exploration, which may be fun for detectives. It also alerts one to the treasure house, from ancient Greece, to the darkest of the dark ages, the Renaissance, early modern times, and the Enlightenment, of parody and out-rageous critique of powerful and respectable institutions, some-times in writing, sometimes in pageantry and theater. The partici-pants in this counterculture included all ranks and classes; Peter the Great's mockeries and spectacles may have inspired scenes in Fourier's *Nouveau Monde Amoureux*. The streams entering the pool of French socialism of the 1840s – including Fourierism and Freemasonry, which is in a sense a parody of the Catholic Church – may not then have seemed so strange to people who were aware of this continuous tradition.

In 1830s and 1840s France: "Socialist ideas appealed to all social groups: artisans, peasants, middle classes and some nobles."[11] Later socialist ideas and practice were also considerably more eclectic than is generally assumed, although after 1917 partisans emphasized "purity" and distinctiveness. For example, Fourier influenced nearly all 19th century socialist movements, including the Russian. By the late 19th century, Shakers in the United States considered themselves part of the "communist" movement. Lenin studied the proposals of the Fabians; he lived in London during their heyday. The United States Socialist Party was catalyzed by Edward Bellamy's *Looking Backward*, a novel that includes Marxist analysis of working class organization, Engels' scenario for non-violent revolution, a Fourierist *phalanstery*, and Saint-Simonian technocratic "industrial armies."

Some scholars have argued that neither Henri-Claude de Saint-Simon nor Fourier was a socialist, and that Considerant's bland blend wasn't socialist either. This is based on two criteria for socialism: equality and abolition of private property. However, there is no technical definition of socialism, and rigid divisions among "socialist," "capitalist," "anarchist," even "fascist" are often insupportable. Jonathan Beecher informs us that the word "socialism," first used in the 1830s, was intended as a contrast to egoism and individualism.[12] A defensible definition of socialist might be: one who seeks to replace *laissez-faire* capitalism (including its props and epicycles) with a system of social and economic planning that aims to increase equality in status, resources, freedom, power, and all the good things that are socially distributed (the latter might include nose jobs, even though noses themselves may be naturally distributed). This concept distinguishes socialism from both fascism and anarchism, and it acknowledges the Enlightenment ideal that all institutions must serve human happiness. A concern for ecology might be added today, providing for long-term well being of the human species.

That said, the compartments need to be broken down, for many features of ideology and practice are common among different isms. Socialism may claim that it alone stands for egalitarianism, yet even its ideals, including Marxism, admit various forms of hierarchy. For a different example, both the philanthropic ethos and its institutions (e.g., self-perpetuating endowment boards) are essentially feudal, yet United States capitalism could hardly function without their services in ameliorating the slips of the invisible hand. Corporatism, in the form of interest group representation, was important to feudalism, fascism, and United States capitalism. Communist systems, like capitalist ones, idealize the traditional family and profess meritocratic allocation of status.

Pre-Marxian Socialism

Socialism's roots are ancient; its elements are found in almost all major religions. Furthermore, the practical examples of medieval monastic communities and those of the Protestant Reformation's left wing were important inspirations for socialism. British contributions were substantial, especially Gerard Winstanley's Digger ethic and Robert Owen's communitarian and cooperative theories. Nevertheless, the French were perhaps the most fertile in early communism and socialism.

The Enlightenment and the French Revolutionary period witnessed a critique of all institutions, and a radical wing took flight. Perhaps best known was François-Noël Babeuf (Gracchus):

> In November [1795] Babeuf published the first in the new genre of social revolutionary manifestos that would culminate in Marx's [sic] *Communist Manifesto* of 1848. Babeuf's *Plebeian Manifesto* was both a philosophical inventory (a *manifest* of what was needed to bring about "equality in fact" and "the common good") and a call for a popular uprising (a *manifestation*, "greater, more solemn, more general than has ever been done before").[13]

He evoked the image of the Greek (military) "phalanx" as the revolutionary agent, denied any right to private property, and called for the equalization of wealth. These were his principles:

- Take from him who has too much, to give to him who has nothing.
- The aim of Society is general happiness.
- The fruits of the earth belong to all, the land to no one.[14]

These ideas exemplified 18th century communism; the word "communism" has been attributed to Restif de la Bretonne, a prolific utopian-pornographic writer of the 1780s.[15] In this early period, "communism" implied a total transformation of institutions, but did not have a special focus on urban working-class struggles.

Freemasonry, in addition to its general influence on the American and French Revolutions, had links with both the revolutionary communist and socialist movements.[16] Felippo Buonarroti, an Italian participant in the Babeuf conspiracy, used the lodges of Geneva as recruiting grounds for communist revolution.

Henri-Claude de Saint Simon (1760-1825) shows the influence of both Jean-Jacques Rousseau and scientific-enlightenment currents; he had close associates in the "Philadelphians" Masonic lodge.[17] He was an important influence throughout the 19th century on the French socialist camp, but can best be seen as a harbinger of "technocracy." The word "socialist" was first used by Owenites in 1827; in French it appeared only in 1832, in the Saint-Simonian newspaper, *Le Globe*.

Saint-Simon claimed to have discovered the science of society. He argued that those who produced wealth should rule, to further the supreme goal of history: the mental and physical betterment of the poorest and most numerous class. Although he regarded this progress to be inevitable, he thought it important to help the process along to insure that it would be orderly and non–violent:

> The supreme law of the human spirit's progress leads and dominates all; men are only instruments of it. . . . All that we can do is obey this law (our true Providence) with knowledge of the cause, understanding the direction it prescribes to us, instead of being pushed blindly by it. . . [18]

His elite would include industrialists, scientists, and artists, as the latter had the role of propagandists for the new system. They were to portray the glories of the future earthly paradise, just as they had formerly depicted the Christian heaven, to remind men of the proper moral direction. Yet Christianity still had a role in promoting industrialization, by creating church-directed enterprises and inspiring the workforce. Saint-Simon had no interest in communitarianism; his utopia was to be the land of abundance, where government would wither away, becoming only the "administration of things," not the control over persons. Exploitation of nature, according to a national plan, would absorb hostile or competitive energies. To avoid war, the European countries should together create great international public works projects, "civilize" and Christianize the "inferior races," and make the world "habitable like Europe."

Saint-Simon's ideas prefigured France's later "state capitalism" practice; his historical theories also influenced the socialist tradition, for example:

> This [feudal-theological] social system had been born during the preceding system [Graeco-Roman] at the very time when that system had attained its highest development. Similarly, when the feudal-theological system was firmly established during the Middle Ages, the germ of its destruction was born, and the elements of the system that must today replace it had just been created.[19]

Charles Fourier, born in 1772 in Besançon, was a brilliant and hilarious critic of post-revolutionary France and just about every institution and theory found therein.[20] Here is Engels' appraisal of him:

> French nonsense is at least cheerful, whereas German nonsense is gloomy and profound. And then, Fourier has criticised existing social relations so sharply, with such wit and humour that one readily forgives him for his cosmological fantasies which are also based on a brilliant world outlook. . . .
>
> Fourier inexorably exposes the hypocrisy of respectable society, the contradiction between its theory and its practice, the dullness of its entire mode of life; he ridicules its philosophy, its striving for *perfecting the perfectibility which is in process of becoming perfect and august truth*, he ridicules its "pure morality," its uniform social institutions, and contrasts all this with its practice, *le doux commerce*, which he criticises in a masterly manner, its dissolute delights which are no delights, its organisation of adultery in marriage, its general chaos.[21]

Fourier was moved by an acute awareness of starvation amongst plenty, the sight of merchants dumping grain into the sea to raise its price, and the corruption he daily witnessed in his own unchosen occupation as a traveling salesman of silk. His bachelor life permitted him to become an autodidact after his *collège* (academic high school) education, and he devoted himself to the study of just about everything, without any of the inhibitions that weigh down respectable scholars. His observations of the working of "free enterprise" were brilliant (as Engels acknowledged). For example, even in his day, agribusiness was imposing a new feudalism on farmers:

> [M]onopolists . . . could reduce all those below them to commercial vassalage, and achieve control over the whole of production by their combined intrigues. The small landowner would then be forced indirectly to dispose of his harvest in a way that met with the monopolists' agreement; he would in fact have become an agricultural agent of the commercial coalition. The final result of this would be the renaissance of an inverse feudalism, founded on mercantile leagues rather than leagues of nobles.[22]

He was also an acute observer (or voyeur) of the contemporary loosening of morals, especially among the presumed respectable classes.

Fourier's studies led him to believe that he had discovered the true science of society – he compared himself to Newton – that would enable everyone to enjoy full expression of all talents, passions, and manias. At the same time, all necessary work would be done and a good time would be had by all. This was because "passionate attraction," the psychological equivalent of gravitation, would motivate both work and play, and harmony (also the name of his ideal society) would result from the unfettered expression of instincts. Even the nastiest of human desires would become harmless through sublimation and playful outlets. For example, the "world war of *petits pâtés*" would enlist 60 armies of men and women on a European battleground, where they would compete to make the best array of these pastries. One million bottles of champagne would be in readiness for the victory party. Excitement would mount as alliances changed daily.[23]

To implement his system, it would be necessary to abandon

individual households (which were in any cases arenas of boredom and oppression) for self-sufficient communities (*phalansteries*)
enrolling all classes and dispositions – variety was essential. These
would provide a generous minimum of food, clothing, lodging,
education, entertainment, medical and dental care, and sex.
Communards would engage in voluntarily chosen and frequently
varied occupations. There would be trade, wild partying, and
joint ventures among *phalansteries*.

Fourier's communitarianism dispenses with nations, armies,
bureaucracies, corporations, marriage, and institutionalized religion. Still, there would be some rules and gentle non-violent
punishments within the *phalanstery*. Organization was necessary
to insure that everyone shared not only in subsistence, but also in
such essentials of the good life as sex, love, and self-esteem. The
community would replace the family and provide a humane,
enlightened, and secure environment for children. Fourier believed that women could be neither free nor equal in the marriage institution; he was the most feminist of early socialists.

Fourier did not call for the total abolition of private property.
He presumed that the *phalanstery* would be super-productive, as
it eliminated waste and duplication and released tremendous energy by passionate attraction. Profits would then be distributed on
the basis of capital (3/12), talent (4/12), and labor (5/12). Thus, he
didn't project an egalitarian future. However, three factors should
be noted about Fourier's concept of distribution. First of all, he
insisted that even the poorest in his "Harmony" would enjoy a
standard of living, both material and cultural, far higher than
that of the typical middle-class person of his day. Second, his
radical hedonism noted that some people derived great pleasure
from conspicuous consumption, or bringing off a sharp deal. His
system would permit these, on the condition that no one would
be hurt by such activities. Third, Fourier's imagination encom-
passed inequalities far broader than those denounced by most
socialists of his day, or even ours. He was concerned about the
creative outlets and sex lives of the elderly; the sexual and social
deprivations of the unattractive and nerdy; everyone's self-esteem
needs; the boredom of much work, regardless of its status or
remuneration; the mean treatment of children, not just those of

the poor; and even the inequalities that exist between capital and provincial cities. He devised institutions to attack all these problems; a brilliant first draft unfortunately rarely followed up by later socialists.

Fourier also eschewed all violence in bringing about socialism. His methods were persuasion, through the written word, lectures, and demonstration communities. He hoped to convert those of all classes, believing that everyone would be better off under his system. In addition to the romantic "utopian" dreams of human happiness, Fourier walked the road of the Enlightenment rationalist tradition. For example, he did not think that an agricultural laboring class was compatible with democracy. Without slavery, peonage, or a peasantry, no one would willingly engage in full time farm service (unlike, e.g. locksmithing or topiary, for which some might have a passion). His rational solution was to have everyone do a little of it, and furthermore, to adopt a diet that avoided the drudgery of field crops or cattle raising. This, based on legumes, vegetables, fruits, and small animals, is perhaps the most healthful anyway. Similarly, the democratic solution for menial work was not to construct a meritocracy, but to make it as attractive as possible through play and flirting opportunities, to employ those with psychological affinities for such work, who could indulge without status considerations, and to share any leftover dangerous or repugnant essential jobs in small doses. Rotation in work would also allow for the full expression of the human personality. He did not abolish expertise; rather, he assumed that those who were highly skilled at some tasks would occupy novice positions when they rotated to other work.

From today's perspective, Fourier was perhaps most prescient in suggesting that in a socialist society, or even any system with democratic pretensions, menial work cannot be the lifelong daily work of a class, a race, a gender, or the unlucky. Our capitalist societies find peons through immigration and female guilt labor; this bounty may not last. Already there are shortages of health care workers, teachers, nurses, and carpenters, and few young people want to be fishmongers, furnace repairpersons, or tailors. The invisible hand is not dealing us what we need. Paradoxically, the Fourierist system, while providing a remedy for unemployment, also serves well for labor shortages.

In addition, demographic changes illuminate the practicality of Fourierism. Declining birth rates (already in evidence in 1840s France) leads to a shortage of laborers; modern medicine and social factors result in a surplus of mate-seeking women, insofar as pairs are still required. Now there are predictions that soon unimaginable numbers of people will live to be 100. Who will take care of them? Their 80-year-old children, if they have any, or any left? Evidence from communitarian societies of the 19th century indicates that the elderly were well cared for in community, as part of the work shared by all. Unfortunately, Fourier's schemes for sharing work were soon laundered out of the socialist ideal.

Fourier believed that marriage, even among the wealthy and well-servanted, was incompatible with women's freedom and equality and must be replaced with more functional institutions. His observations of the real world led him to believe that monogamy was a rare mania – to be permitted, of course, in his *phalanstery* – but inappropriate as a norm. He was also concerned with the harm inflicted on children in most traditional, as well as disintegrated families. Today, worldwide, the "traditional" family is a minority configuration, yet our informal alternatives may not incorporate the security, or fun, that the *phalanstery* was designed to provide, to say nothing of the enormous burden that still falls on women.

In addition to his many brilliant suggestions, Fourier had weird ideas about planets copulating, seas turning into lemonade, and anti-lions, to which Engels had referred. Both his chief United States popularizer, Albert Brisbane, and Considerant did their best to suppress these as well as his wild (but non-violent) sexual schemes. Fourier in person was also a public relations liability, and his disciples tried to maneuver him out of sight. When Considerant, one year before the master's death, became the full-time interpreter of Fourierism, it underwent a major transformation.

Etienne Cabet (1788-1856) was influenced by Owen and Chartists during his exile in England, and shared the French communists' goals of abolishing of private property and equalizing wealth, yet he rejected violent revolution. The major exposition of his doctrine, *Voyage en Icarie* (1840) describes a communitarian utopia; he had a large working-class following.

Another important figure in the French 1840s radical scene was Pierre-Joseph Proudhon (1809–1865). Born in Besançon, like Fourier, he had come across Fourier's *Nouveau Monde Industriel et Sociétaire* (1829) as its typesetter, and read it with great interest. Yet his ideas were more in the tradition of Jean-Jacques Rousseau. He envisioned a social system that would be a federation of small patriarchal farms and workshops, along with cooperative commercial establishments. Although he is well known for his slogan "Property is theft," he aimed at only certain types of property: that of big capitalists and banks.

Considerant and Fourierism

Victor Considerant was born in Salins (Jura) in 1808, and attended the same *collège* in Besançon as had Fourier. During these years he learned of Fourierism from two local followers: Just Muiron, a local government official, and Clarisse Vigoureux, a wealthy widow, his future mother–in-law. Considerant continued his education at the *École Polytechnique* in Paris, where he studied engineering. Here the ideas of Henri-Claude de Saint-Simon were in vogue, and Considerant became well acquainted with them. Like many of his fellow students, he joined the military engineering corps upon graduation in 1830. By then, he was already a Fourier publicist, and in 1836 he gave up his career to become Fourier's full-time disciple and interpreter.

Considerant followed his master in seeking harmony and class collaboration, and rejecting violence and radical equalization of property. They were both outraged at the consequences of a "free enterprise" system, which was creating poverty among rural and urban workers, constant insecurity for the middle class, and a new aristocracy of monopolists and speculators. It was not coincidental that Considerant was an engineer; those so trained were receptive to planning and formed an important core of nineteenth century French socialism.

Although Considerant revered science, he also had faith in human goodness and Jesus' message of love. In contrast, Fourier's religion had been his own version of deism: passionate attraction was God's plan for humanity's salvation. Understanding this, as Fourier did, "social scientists" could transform disruptive passions into harmony. Considerant suggests a Christian socialist approach, one of his radical emendations of Fourier.

Considerant continued to publish detailed expositions of the *phalanstery*, which had been an important recruitment tool. Nevertheless, in his popular presentations, he increasingly de-emphasized all but its economic virtues. This eliminated the shocking and fantastic elements, but also much of Fourier's brilliant social criticism. Socialism as a product of the Enlightenment aimed at all the institutions stifling human happiness and well being, including war, status distinctions, slavery, political oppression, organized religion, marriage, and fashion, in addition to irrational and oppressive economic systems. Much of Fourier's *oeuvre* parodies these institutions; hardly any of this remains in the sober Considerant. Perhaps the most striking omission was his evisceration of Fourier's radical feminism. Considerant did support women's suffrage, yet his heart does not seem to have been in it.

The strange twist that gave Fourierism its opportunity was that in the 1820s some self-proclaimed leaders of the originally technocratic Saint-Simonian movement adopted cultish and bizarre practices and notions, such as a search for a female Messiah. Saint-Simonianism had a large following by 1831 (approximately 40,000) when massive defections to Fourierism began, especially among the engineers and other practically minded adherents.[24] What they saw of Fourierism, thanks to the way it had been pitched by Considerant and other publicists, was the *phalanstery* as a practical plan for the amelioration of poverty and unemployment. ". . . [T]he *phalanstery* seemed more like a model farm or an agricultural colony founded by a philanthropic association rather than the basic building block of Harmony."[25] It is possible that the transformation of Fourierism was abetted by technological changes. Just as Ebenezer Howard's late 19th century charming and rational Garden City schemes were ultimately derailed by the private automobile, the thrill of railroads in the 1840s sidetracked the *phalanstery* in favor of national planning bureaucracies.

During the 1830s and 1840s, Fourierist societies (latitudinarian in doctrine) gained thousands of followers in France, Belgium, and Switzerland. There were headquarters in Paris, many provincial branches, a daily newspaper, a theoretical journal, pamphlets, a bookstore, and regular banquets, including special ones on Fourier's birthday. "Finally, on April 7, 1847, Fourier's seventy-fifth birthday was celebrated in thirty-four French cities and towns (also New York City, Rio de Janeiro, and Mauritius)." [26] "Under Considerant's leadership, the École sociétaire, the official Fourierist society, organized branch societies in almost every major city in Europe and in the United States and disseminated propaganda throughout the world." [27]

Why did so many join this movement? They were professionals (lawyers, doctors, architects, engineers), military officers, students, small businesspeople, artists, musicians, journalists, and artisans. They probably had adequate food (or excellent in France, where restaurants had been recently invented because when aristocrats lost their heads, their cooks no longer had mouths to feed), sex (also possibly better in France due to widespread use of birth control), and warm houses. In the United States, an "American Union of Associationists" was formed, comprising local and regional groups, and at least 100,000 interested followers. [28]

Socialism provided a new worldview to replace Catholicism. Fourierism's claim to be a "social science" gave it Enlightenment credentials; paradoxically, its newly acquired Christian socialist perspective offered religious inspiration and consolation. Although the new capitalists attributed poverty and increasing economic distress to "laziness and immorality," many people believed that something was wrong with the economic system. The advent of large-scale industrial capitalism was seen especially threatening to small businesses, farmers, and skilled craftspeople. Unlike Icarian communism, Fourierism was a "cross-class" solution, promising to unite rich, middle, and poor. This characteristic was especially attractive to recruits from Freemasonry, which had similar goals.

As with all radical movements, there were personal reasons for adherence. The Fourierists recruited from the disintegrating Saint-Simonians, which drew a large number of engineers, who, like Considerant, had discussed these doctrines while at the École Polytechnique. For them, social engineering in accordance with

Fourier's complex numerical formula had a particular attraction. In addition, many shared the experience of Nicolas Lemoyne, who, upon graduation, was assigned to supervise rather boring provincial road building projects. These engineers believed themselves part of an elite, yet they had no power or status, and lacked even the exciting conversations of their school days.[29] Other Saint-Simonians moving on to Fourierism were Jews— Considerant avoided publicizing Fourier's anti-Semitism—and women, often highly educated, but lacking status in French society. Considerant himself had been recruited by his future mother-in-law, Clarisse Vigoureux.

Doctors and educators were impressed with Fourier's quite rational medical and educational theories. Labor organizers and people in the incipient "helping professions" were interested. Some wealthy philanthropists liked the idea of engaging in "social engineering" rather than simply giving their money to charity.[30] Finally, there were those who thought creating overseas Fourierist communities would be a useful instrument of colonialism; this was true of British Fourierists as well.

Considerant lectured, wrote, and edited publications; popularizations of Fourier's ideas sold well, even among working class readers. However, he showed little enthusiasm for creating a trial *phalanstery*, although other Fourierists attempted this in France (1832 and 1841) and Algeria (1845), without much success. The United States was a more fertile ground, and scores of experiments in Fourierism ensued, stimulated especially by Brisbane's expositions in *The Social Destiny of Man, or Association and Reorganization of Industry* (Philadelphia, 1840), pamphlets, and a purchased front-page daily column in the *New York Tribune* (1842-1843).[31]

By the mid-1830s, Considerant began to regard working class movements and electoral politics as the paths to reform. His journalism and practical activities were moving in this new direction; nevertheless, he continued to work on his massive exposition of Fourier doctrine: *Destinée sociale,* published in three volumes between 1834 and 1844. In 1843 he was elected to the Parisian local government council, and in the same year, he transformed the Fourierist journal, *La Phalange,* into a new daily newspaper,

La Démocratie pacifique. This was designed as an organ for a political socialist movement, shorn of all Fourierist peculiarities. Considerant wrote his *Manifeste* for the 1843 introductory issue of the newspaper; it was reprinted as a pamphlet in 1847.

La Démocratie pacifique was a general newspaper, with advertisements, theater listings, crime reports, and much commentary on current news; its circulation reached 2,200.[32] At that time, such newspapers were a new development, and their survival depended on donations from enthusiasts. It still championed the idea of "association," yet the *phalanstery* as the road to socialism was soft-pedaled in favor of broad "New Deal-like" state action, including guarantees of the right to work, public works projects, and central economic planning. Even the term *phalanstery* was omitted in favor of "*commune*," meaning "town" (without any of the later hippie connotations).[33]

The 1848 Revolution lent Considerant great hope that his theories might be realized; he contested and won a seat in the National Assembly. He then served on committees devoted to the unemployment crisis, yet he had no success in either advancing reformist goals or spreading the Fourierist word. His continued condemnation of the Communist tendency, for both its methods and goals, kept him apart from the working class.

Considerant played a major role in an 1849 protest action against the Government's plan to engineer a regime change for the Roman Republic. The insurrection was put down, some violence ensued, and he was forced to flee, becoming an exile in Belgium. There he decided that it might be a propitious time for a trial *phalanstery*. After meeting with Brisbane, he went to the United States and visited the North American Phalanx and Oneida communities. In 1852, he arrived in Texas, a land he found promising.

In 1855, Considerant bought land near Dallas, intending to create a colony that would host various communal experiments, not only Fourierist ones. The preparation had been inadequate, and the environment hostile both physically and politically. Nevertheless, colonists began arriving from France, including children, elderly, and inappropriately skilled. Considerant was inept as an administrator, despite his military engineering education, and the colony disintegrated amidst acrimony and lack of hominy (malnutrition). He then moved to San Antonio, where he farmed, collected cacti, and sat out the Civil War. Upon his return to France in 1869, he was still celebrated by the surviving Fourierists. By then he had been influenced by Social Darwinism, and advocated a federated Europe, in concert with the United States, to serve as a benevolent world government. He kept his faith in socialism and pacifism.

The Tradition of "Manifestos"

Babeuf's, Considerant's, and *The Communist Manifesto* (in English translation) are now available in full text online, including Engels' early drafts of the *CM*. Considerant shares with Babeuf one major premise: "The aim of society is general happiness." However, he rejects Babeuf's demand to confiscate property, abolish property rights, legislate absolute equality, and use violent means to bring about the communist realm.

Considerant's *Manifeste* begins with a reminder of Saint-Simon's periodization of history, and his idea that the economically dominant group writes the laws and dominates all aspects of society. This is surprising because Considerant's master, Charles Fourier, had a totally different concept of historical stages, not at all materialist but based on the degree of self-knowledge attained. The *Manifeste* is indeed heavily imbued with Saint-Simonianism, and is intended to unite "all men of good will" in an eclectic moderate socialist movement. Considerant argues that all classes are hurt by capitalism; thus, all should work for its demise. He describes the growing class war, but rejects it as an instrument of salvation. Rather, he insists on the urgent need for reform and replacement of the laissez-faire system. This must be accomplished while preserving unequal property, rights to inheritance, a social Christianity, and the traditional family.

The *Communist Manifesto* was written partly in response to Considerant's.[34] The initial premises of both are similar, with references to the Saint-Simonian materialist periodization of history. The depredations of capitalism and the growing class struggle are described. However, unlike Considerant, Marx and Engels find many virtues in capitalism's "civilizing" march through the earth. Considerant is happy to be rid of feudalism, but believed that a new system had to be put in its place; capitalism destroys all, even the capitalists themselves. The *Communist Manifesto* notes the role that the bourgeoisie play in educating the proletariat to their revolutionary task; this creates some inconsistency with their other assertions that consciousness is determined by class position. On the other hand, Considerant has no doubt that an enlightened elite must lead the way and serve as the people's guardians until they are adequately educated for full political participation.

There is a vast difference between his advocacy of peaceful reform, initiated perhaps by parliament or king, and the call to violent revolution of the *Communist Manifesto.* The latter document also seeks to discredit all competing parties and ideologies, while Considerant revels in eclecticism, and pays homage to all, even proponents of the *Ancien Régime.*

Despite the self-identification of Marx and Engels with the "communist" movement, their practical proposals for social reconstruction owed more to the utopians. At the end of Section II of the *Communist Manifesto* Marx and Engels sketch an immediate post-revolutionary program; in items 5-10, we can see Considerant's influence:

5. Centralization of credit in the banks of the state, by means of a national bank with state capital and an exclusive monopoly.

6. Centralization of the means of communication and transport in the hands of the state.

7. Extension of factories and instruments of production owned by the state; the bringing into cultivation of waste lands, and the improvement of the soil generally in accordance with a common plan.

8. Equal obligation of all to work. Establishment of industrial armies, especially for agriculture.

9. Combination of agriculture with manufacturing industries; gradual abolition of the distinction between town and country by a more equable distribution of the populace over the country.

10. Free education for all children in public schools. Abolition

of children's factory labor in its present form. Combination
of education with industrial production, etc.

In the later works of Marx and Engels, although socialist goals
are quite vague, there is little support for the Babouvian vision of
an austere, agrarian, egalitarian future, or the abolition of progress,
enlightenment, and meritocracy that it implied.

Freemasonry and Socialism

In early 19th Century France, many regarded socialism as a
logical extension of the Enlightenment and democratic reform.
These were mainly middle class, with roots in provincial France,
who eschewed class struggle and violent revolution. Often, men
with such views were Freemasons, and some lodges designated
themselves Fourierist or Saint-Simonian.

In recent years Freemasonry has received attention from
social scientists, which makes its study more accessible and respectable. A major question in the current debate is whether
Freemasonry has promoted democracy, or rather has been racist
and sexist, repressive to working class organization, and/or an
accessory to imperialism.[35] Such issues matter, as Masonry has had
a great impact on history and politics worldwide, and has occupied, along with cognate organizations, large areas of "civil society." Masonic influence was also significant in United States
communitarian socialism, including Mormonism, which has sometimes been regarded as a derivative of Freemasonry.

Freemasonry had been an important component of the Enlightenment and the French Revolution. It rivaled and sought to
displace the discredited Catholic Church, supplying its own ethics,
rituals, and buildings. The lodges were male-only clubs, despite a
few examples of "androgynous Masonry."[36] For ruling class Masons, such as Frederick the Great, Napoleon Bonaparte, and
Louis-Philippe (the "bourgeois" King of the French July Monarchy), it was a vehicle for anti-clericalism and modernization. The
French Masonic-socialist connection was fostered by a convergence
of ideology. In addition, government repression of openly political organizations during the 1840s made the lodges convenient
places to foment socialism.

Political discussion in the French Masonic lodges of the 1840s was mostly about socialism of one type or another, with the principles of "*sociabilité* and association" receiving general approval as the bases for social reform.[37] Many of the leading socialists were Masons, including Considerant, François Cantagrel, and Proudhon.[38]

> Going back to the 1840s, Fourierism has been an important player in converting French revolutionists into reformist freemasons. In France of that period, relatively many radical and progressive people were joining freemasonry, converting it into a political voluntary organization and fixing its grand view as fighting for the democratization of France by non-violent methods.[39]

However, in addition to the socialists, there were Freemasons concerned about poverty who held a traditional charitable approach, and saw "model farms" as a solution for the poor, rather than "*phalansteries*" changing all classes' entire ways of life.

Fourier was not a Freemason, although he was clearly influenced by Masonry. There had been a French lodge called *Harmonie*, and throughout Europe, "androgynous" lodges, some with risqué rituals that would not have been surprising in Fourier's *Nouveau Monde Amoureux*. In *Theory of Four Movements*, Fourier suggested that Freemasonry could become the transitional form to his ideal society. It had a network, religious trappings, secret meetings, and a well-off membership, which made it attractive to the aspiring classes, and all it needed was the introduction of "women and sensual pleasure."[40] Notwithstanding, Freemasonry developed as an all–male institution, with "ladies' auxiliaries," thereby reinforcing the marginalization of women in both modern democracies and French socialism. One Masonic–inspired organization that came close to Fourierist prescriptions was the United States Granger movement (Patrons of Husbandry) organized in 1868 by Oliver Kelley. The Grange had social, educational, and political aspects; it was the first farm organization in which women participated as full members. Kelley, a Mason, incorporated rituals and solidarity values into the Grange. While sex orgies may or may not have been common, to Fourier, a fine Granger apple pie would have been a major pleasure.

French Politics in the 1840s

A variety of governmental forms followed the French Revolution of 1789, unsatisfactory to both those who wanted to increase democratization and those who wanted to restore the *ancien régime*. In addition, there was increasing concern about rural and urban economic problems that governments had failed to address. For example, the industrialization of the textile industry was causing considerable distress. In Lyons, convent-workshops operated by the Catholic Church used children to weave silk; skilled artisans could not compete with this arrangement.[41]

In July 1830, the reign of the reactionary Bourbon Charles X was ended by revolution, and Louis Philippe, of the Orleanist line, was installed as a constitutional monarch. From 1830 to 1848, the government was known as the "July Monarchy." Although there was an elected Chamber of Deputies, the franchise was very limited. Only one in 30 or 40 (depending on sources) adult males could vote, and the government was essentially a plutocracy, amenable to the bribery of the canal and railway corporations and large banks. There were no formal political parties; however, there were several factions in the legislature. The opposition included both republicans and monarchists desiring a broader franchise, and those seeking restoration of the Bourbons and Catholic Church; no socialists were in parliament during this period. The majority faction was headed by François Guizot, who accepted the general results of the French Revolution, but did not want democratization beyond the 1830 arrangements; he was usually identified as a conservative. Frequent bribery scandals, non-recognition of widespread social and economic distress, and policies favoring big business aroused Considerant's ire, although he had some sympathy with Guizot's belief that the suffrage should be based on capacity. Nevertheless, Considerant thought far more should be done to educate the masses for political competence. He also shared Guizot's reluctance to engage in democracy promotion through violent intervention in other countries, which many republicans were demanding.

By 1848, the Orleanist monarchy had lost much support, and the opposition, consisting of republicans seeking political reform, middle and working class socialists (especially in Paris and Lyons), and generally disgruntled workers and peasants, ignited another revolution. Considerant was elected to the Chamber of Deputies in the ensuing short-lived Second Republic, ended by a coup of Louis Napoleon in 1851. Socialism continued as an underground movement, often in the Masonic lodges, and had some influence on policies of the Third Republic, proclaimed in 1870.[42]

Considerant's "Peaceful Socialism" and Feminism, Environmentalism, Colonialism, and Atheism

The *Manifeste* gives no comfort to feminism; it is addressed to men only. In other writings of this period, Considerant argued for women's rights in marriage, divorce reform, educational and professional opportunities, and even the right to vote. However, he abjures the radical feminism of Fourier, who posited the intellectual superiority of women, advocated their total sexual liberation, and desired the abolition of the family because it restricted sexual choice, confined women (even rich ones) to domestic tasks, and wasn't even good for the children. When his opponents reminded Considerant of Fourier's shocking doctrines, he dodged the issue, claiming that it was a ridiculous charge. He retorted that his perspective was the moral one: that the greatest immorality was forcing people to stay married when they either never loved each other, or no longer did so. This yoking is "slavery of the heart," itself the worst form of adultery, and causes all the miseries, abandoned seduced women, abandoned children, false paternity, lies and hypocrisy.[43] Essentially, he was upholding the system of "serial monogamy" that Engels later advocated, which works like "laissez-faire" in the sexual market-place.

Fourier had extolled the economic and liberatory benefits of collective households; Considerant makes only a casual reference to them in an 1848 publication.[44] However, as early as 1838, he referred to marriage in his ideal society as a freely entered contract, in place of "infeudation" of the wife to the husband. Economic guarantees were to be based in "*communes*" (towns); *phalansteries* were already fading from the picture.[45]

Women were never accepted as equals in the Fourierist movement; their writings were published in the journals, but they were not invited to be speakers on Fourierist platforms. Flora Tristan was even excluded from the annual Fourierist banquet on account of her sex.[46] Although apparently a faithful husband, Considerant didn't share the intellectual or organizational work with the two very intelligent Fourierist women in his household: his wife and his mother-in-law (who was the moneybags).

Considerant's normalizing of Fourier eliminated the environmental benefits of largely self-sufficient communities, employing appropriate technology, and producing for need (not jobs or profits). In Fourier's vision, the collective household was expected to permit vast savings in resources and energy use, along with a greatly improved quality of life. "[T]hree hundred families of associated villagers need have only one well-ordered granary, instead of three hundred ill-kept ones; only one wine-vat instead of three hundred . . ."[47] The benefits of combined creativity and knowledge would also be considerable even for the rich:

> In the current order [it is necessary] for every head of household to know about oenology, knowledge which is not easy to acquire. Three-quarters of rich households lack this knowledge, and consequently are very poorly stocked with wine; they spend a lot of money on drink, but have nothing but adulterated and badly kept wines because they have to rely on wine-merchants who are the most adept swindlers and on hired cellarmen whose only skill is cheating. [48]

Today, we may not be so concerned with wine-vats or butlers, but socialists must face the question of how to universalize a "Western" standard of living. Is every household in the world to possess a SUV, HDTV, exercise bicycle, and all the other delights of modern technology? If not (for environmental as well as economic reasons), how can we deny them these pleasures, while we are wallowing in Viking King ranges, spray-steam irons, and Jacuzzis? The Fourierist solution is to live lightly but well on the earth by sharing luxuries, in contrast to the austere visions of most other "utopians." Another argument for collective households is that today, despite modern gadgets, managing a household for maximum health and well being requires time and knowledge. For example, preparation of nutritious and delicious meals, avoidance of toxic materials, and non-oppressive child raising are still great challenges. Standards have been declining in many departments, because most information about how to live comes from advertising, and competing sources have been weakened: traditional wisdom, home economics classes, and even the influence of savvy servants and cellarmen. With all adults working outside the home, the core – heart or hearth – may soon rot.

Considerant gradually departed from the Fourierist vision, very much in the spirit of Saint-Simon, and argued that transforming nature is the way to provide for well being, eliminate poverty, and discharge aggressions. Not unexpectedly considering his engineering background, he also admired massive projects as expressions of human genius. Nevertheless, he did not share Saint-Simon's endorsement of colonialism or the exploitation of the non-European world. (True to his theory but inadvertently, his colony in Texas hardly transformed anything.) In this regard, he was more anti-colonialist than Marx and Engels, whose *Manifesto* tends to regard these developments as progressive.

Considerant proposed a federation of European nations employing international law and conciliation to preserve the peace; his pacifism was also important protection for the environment. One commentator on Fourier's "industrial armies" (international work brigades) noted:

> The expenditure, he points out with the logic of a commercial traveller, would be much smaller for a productive army; and besides the saving in slaughtered men, burnt cities, devastated fields, we should have the saving of the cost of equipment, and the benefit of the work accomplished.[49]

Considerant evolved into a Christian socialist, not an unusual stance for the mid-19th century, when Deism among radicals and socialists was being replaced by something like liberation theology. He increasingly identified socialism with the "spirit of Jesus," and although this was probably a sincere conversion, it also made his doctrines far more appealing to both working and middle classes. Engels complained that even the Communists (i.e., Icarians) in

France were Christians, who insisted that "Christianity is Communism."[50]

Implications for "Third Way" Theory

What can today's searchers for alternatives to Marxism, capitalism, and globalism learn from the Considerant *Manifeste*, and early French socialism more generally?

A. Economic and political democracy are not necessarily aligned; universal suffrage may co-exist with plutocracy, military adventurism, imperialism, and demagoguery. The experience of the Athenian democracy may still be valid. A popularly based imperialism can exploit the world's resources for the benefit of capitalists and proletarians in the wealthier nations.

Considerant was concerned that the electorate would destroy democracy without resolving the economic crisis; the election of Louis Napoleon confirmed his fears.

B. The proletariat as agent for communist revolution has shrunk in the capitalist nations. This occurred not only because of automation, but also because to some extent, Marx's was a self-denying prophecy. Unemployment was seen as dangerous, and consequently, work has been provided through government employment (as Roberto Michels suggested), including warriors directly hired and subcontracted, and a large non–profit sector (especially in the US, where many social services have long been privatized). Even in manufacturing industries, many blue collar jobs have been supplanted by service occupations: government relations, public relations, athletic director for staff, real estate dealer, art director for headquarters building, environmental manager, sensitivity trainer, etc. Those actually unemployed may be mollified by government benefits or help from the non-profit sector; they may also undertake small businesses, legal or illegal, often off the books. So where are the troops for the working class revolution?

C. It is not easy to interest the industrial working class in socialism. As in Considerant's day, private property remains attractive to many, not only in the form of home ownership (as in the United States), but also small businesses and farms, however inefficient and oppressive. Even in the most solidly Communist enclave in the capitalist world, Bologna, Italy, for decades loyal Communist voters were happy owners of small businesses, such as food processing and equipment, which may have involved peppers, but were neither green nor red.

D. Socialist and communist movements have been important components of national liberation struggles, but in the developed West, they have been weak on political sociology and psychology. European working class socialists were often motivated by the desire for a decent life, and when Keynesian measures appeared to provide some security, they became less interested in abolishing capitalism. On the other hand, middle class socialists were often attracted to "romantic" or "utopian" aspects of socialism, the need for a comprehensive worldview to replace Christianity, or the desire for a just, rational, and more ecological economic system. They were uncomfortable with a prosperity that was dependent on international exploitation or risked world war, and weren't acting to improve their economic status, although low social status may have been a spur – as with women, Jews, the disabled, and underemployed intellectuals.

Too much faith has been placed in Marxist assumptions in regard to agency, and too little critique has been directed at Marxist prescriptions for transforming the earth, or its suggestion that imperialism is progressive (i.e., is helping to move nations towards the ultimate revolution). Violent revolution in well-fortified capitalist democracies is not only unlikely to succeed; its consequences may be disastrous. Victory of the proletariat through election is now nearly impossible; in any case, capital flight would occur as soon as such a development became a possibility. It may be that the only way to attain any system change is through negotiation and compromise among all classes, and/or by means of small-scale cooperative ventures that might possibly survive in a world of megacorporations.

Notes

1. Among those who have made such accusations are George Sorel and W. Techerkesoff. Reported in Rondel V. Davidson, "Reform versus Revolution: Victor Considerant and the *Communist Manifesto,*" *Social Science Quarterly* 58 (1): 74-85, 1977.

2. The *Manifeste* referred to in the quotation is the 1843 edition,

appearing as the introduction to Considerant's new journal, *Démocratie pacifique.* Jonathan Beecher, *Victor Considerant and the Rise and Fall of French Romantic Socialism* (Berkeley: University of California Press, 2001), 163.

3. Davidson, "Reform."

4. There has been an Italian translation, and a Spanish translation is online: http://www.antorcha.net/biblioteca_virtual/politica/manifiesto/considerant.html#47

5. Availableat:http://gallica.bnf.fr/scripts/ConsultationTout.exe?E=0&O =N005455. Of course, for an accurate appraisal, the French *Manifeste* should be compared to the original German *Communist Manifesto.*

6. See the work of André Gorz, e.g., *Farewell to the Working Class* (Boston: South End Press, 1982); Laclau/Mouffe, "Post-Marxism without Apologies," *New Left Review* No. 166, Nov/Dec 1987: 79-106.

7. See Michèle Riot-Sarcey, *Le réel de l'utopie: Essai sur le politique au XIXe siècle* (Paris: Albin Michel, 1998); Louis Ucciani, "Un Regard moderne sur la philosophie de Fourier," (Review of François Dagognet, *Trois philosophies revisitées: Saint-Simon, Proudhon, Fourier* [Hildesheim: Georg Olms, 1997]), *Cahiers Charles Fourier* No. 8, 1997: 91-101.

8. Karl Marx and Frederick Engels, *The Communist Manifesto* (New York: International Publishers, 1948), 31.

9. "An Introduction to the Situationist International," *NB!* #6, 1984. Available: http://www.notbored.org/intro.html.

10. Beecher, *Victor Considerant,* 150.

11. Pamela Pilbeam, *French Socialists Before Marx* (Montreal: McGill-Queen's University Press, 2000), 6.

12. Beecher, *Victor Considerant,* 2.

13. James H. Billington, *Fire in the Minds of Men: Origins of the Revolutionary Faith* (New York: Basic, 1980), 74-5.

14. "Ôter à celui qui a trop, pour donner à celui qui n'a rien. Le but de la Société est le bonheur commun. Les fruits sont à tous, la terre n'est à personne" *Manifeste des Plébéiens,* in *Le Tribune du Peuple,* 1795, p. 256, available at Gallica: http://gallica.bnf.fr.

15. Billington, *Fire,* 7.

16. Billington, *Fire,* 87.

17. Billington, *Fire,* 211.

18. ". . .la loi supériéure des progrès de l'esprit humain entraîne et domine tout; les hommes ne sont pour elle que des instruments. . . . Tout ce que nous pouvons, c'est d'obéir à cette loi (notre véritable Providence) avec connaissance de cause, en nous rendant compte de la marche qu'elle nous prescrit, au lieu d'être poussés aveuglément par elle. . ." Henri-Claude de Saint-Simon, *L'Organisateur,* 1819-1820, In *Oeuvres de Saint-Simon,* Vol. XX, (Paris, 1869), 119. Available: http://gallica.bnf.fr.

19. "Ce système social avait pris naissance pendant la durée du système precedent et même à l'époque où celui-ci venait d'atteindre son développment intégral. Pareillement, lorsque le système féodal et

théologique s'est constitué au moyen âge, la germe de sa destruction commençait a naître, les éléments du système qui doit le remplacer aujourd'hui venaient d'être créés." Saint-Simon, 80.

20. Developments in the publishing and scholarly world have also encouraged a new appraisal of Fourier. Between 1966-8, Éditions Anthropos, Paris, published the *Oeuvres complètes* of Fourier in 12 volumes, which included the first publication of *Le nouveau monde amoureux,* now available as a separate paperback edited by Simone Debout-Oleszkiewicz (Paris: Éditions Stock, 1999). Selections from these volumes were translated and introduced in *The Utopian Vision of Charles Fourier: Selected Texts on Work, Love, and Passionate Attraction,* by Jonathan Beecher and Richard Bienvenu (Boston: Beacon, 1971). Beecher went on to write a masterful biography of Fourier, *Charles Fourier: The Visionary and His World* (Berkeley: University of California Press, 1986); and then of Considerant, *Victor Considerant and the Rise and Fall of French Romantic Socialism* (Berkeley: University of California Press, 2001). Another selection from the *OC* was translated by Susan Hanson and edited by Mark Poster, *Harmonian Man: Selected Writings of Charles Fourier* (Garden City: Anchor Books, 1971). In 1996, Gareth Stedman Jones and Ian Patterson produced a new edition and translation of Fourier's *The Theory of the Four Movements* (Cambridge: Cambridge University Press, 1996). *Cahiers Charles Fourier* (an annual review) began publication in 1990. Edited in Besançon, Fourier's birthplace, this publication unites the small international group pursuing Fourier studies. A brief exposition of Fourierism from a Red-Green perspective is Joan Roelofs, "Charles Fourier: Proto-red-green," in David Macauley (ed.), *Minding Nature: The Philosophers of Ecology* (New York: Guilford, 1996). Currently, the writings of Fourier and Considerant are available for free download from the BNF's Gallica web site.

21. Frederick Engels, "A Fragment of Fourier's on Trade," *Marx Engels Collected Works,* Vol. 4, 613, 1846. Available: http://marxists.org/archive/marx/works/1845/09/fourier.htm

22. Charles Fourier, *The Theory of the Four Movements,* translated and edited by Gareth Stedman Jones and Ian Patterson (Cambridge: Cambridge University Press, 1996), 264.

23. Charles Fourier, *Le Nouveau Monde Amoureux,* ed. Simone Debout-Oleszkiewicz (Paris: Éditions Stock, 1999), 347ff.

24. Billington, *Fire,* 217.

25. ". . . la phalange apparaît parfois davantage comme une ferme-modèle ou comme une colonie agricole fondée par une association philanthropique que comme l'unité élémentaire d'Harmonie." Bernard Desmars, "Être Fouriériste en province: Nicolas Lemoyne, propagandiste du phalanstère," *Cahiers Charles Fourier,* No. 7, 1996, 59.

26. Beecher, *Victor Considerant,* 108.

27. Davidson, "Reform," 76.

28. Carl Guarneri, *The Utopian Alternative: Fourierism in Nine-*

teenth-Century America (Ithaca: Cornell University Press, 1991), 60, 76. See this work for more information on motives in the United States.

29. Desmars, "Être Fouriériste," 48.

30. Guarneri, *Utopian,* 88.

31. Guarneri, *Utopian.*

32. Beecher, *Victor Considerant,* 105.

33. The United States New Deal also had its phalanstery aspects. The Resettlement Administration created communities for the displaced and unemployed, staffed by salaried doctors and traditional crafts instructors. The best known was Jersey Homesteads (later renamed Roosevelt, NJ), which was certainly full of combinations and manias. See Paul Conkin, *Tomorrow a New World: The New Deal Community Program* (Ithaca: Cornell University Press, 1959).

34. Billington, *Fire,* 261.

35. See Mary Ann Clawson, *Constructing Brotherhood: Class, Gender and Fraternalism* (Princeton: Princeton University Press, 1989).

36. For a description of androgynous Masonry of the 18th and 19th centuries, see Charles William Heckethorn, *The Secret Societies of All Ages and Countries,* Vol. II (New Hyde Park: University Books, 1965), 84-90.

37. Avner Halpern, *The Democratisation of France* (London: Minerva, 1999). Available: http://www.geocities.com/SoHo/Den/2479/

38. Philip Nord "Republicanism and the Utopian Vision: French Freemasonry in the 1860s and 1870s," *Journal of Modern History* 63, 1991: 213-29.

39. Personal correspondence, e-mail, Nov. 26, 2003 from Avner Halpern.

40. *Theory of Four Movements,* 197.

41. Laura S. Strumingher, " 'A Bas les Prêtres! A Bas les Couvents!': The Church and the Workers in 19th Century Lyon," *Journal of Social History* 11 (4), 1978: 546-553.

42. Nord, "Republicanism," 229.

43. Victor Considerant, *Le Socialisme devant le vieux monde, ou les vivant devant les morts* (Paris: Librairie Phalanstérienne, 1848), 113. Available: http://gallica.bnf.fr

44. Considerant, *Le Socialisme devant,* 73.

45. Considerant, *Destinée sociale,* Vol. 1 (Paris: Bureau de la Phalange, 1838), 214-216. Available: http://gallica.bnf.fr.

46. Beecher, *Victor Considerant,* 157.

47. *Theory of Four Movements,* 11.

48. *Theory of Four Movements,* 123.

49. David Zeldin, *The Educational Ideas of Charles Fourier* (New York: Kelley, 1969), 109.

50. Frederick Engels, "Progress of Social Reform on the Continent," 1843. Available: http://www.marxists.org.

PRINCIPES

DU

SOCIALISME

MANIFESTE

DE LA

DÉMOCRATIE AU XIX SIÈCLE.

PAR

V. CONSIDÉRANT,

Ancien élève de l'École Polytechnique, membre du conseil général de la Seine.

SUIVI DU

PROCÈS DE LA DÉMOCRATIE PACIFIQUE.

Réimpression de l'édition
Paris 1847

OTTO ZELLER · OSNABRÜCK 1978

Pages from the Paris 1847 edition as reprinted by Otto Zeller, 1978.

MANIFESTE DE LA DÉMOCRATIE.

PREMIÈRE PARTIE.

ÉTAT DE LA SOCIÉTÉ.

—

I. — DES INTÉRÊTS ET DES BESOINS DE LA SOCIÉTÉ.

I.

L'ordre antique et l'ordre féodal.

LES Sociétés de l'antiquité avaient pour principe et pour droit la Force, pour politique la Guerre, pour but la Conquête, et pour système économique l'Esclavage, c'est-à-dire l'exploitation de l'homme par l'homme dans sa forme la plus complète, la plus inhumaine, la plus barbare. L'homme libre, plébéien ou patricien, faisait la guerre et consommait : le producteur était esclave. L'ESCLAVAGE était le fait de base, et le fait culminant la GUERRE. Le sentiment humain ne s'étendait d'ailleurs pas hors des limites de la Patrie. A l'extérieur, la domination implacable de la Patrie sur les peuples étrangers ; à l'intérieur l'esclavage et l'esprit de caste : — Tels étaient les caractères de l'ordre social antique.

L'ordre féodal, résultat de la conquête, n'a été que la conquête organisée. Son fait capital était encore la guerre, et surtout la consécration traditionnelle et permanente des privilèges primitifs de la conquête.

Il avait pour système économique un degré déjà moins dur et moins brutal de l'exploitation de l'homme par l'homme,

Page 1. See p. 47 in this edition.

2

le Servage. Le sentiment humain, s'ouvrant à la chaleur des premiers rayons du Christianisme, sortait des bornes étroites de la Patrie. Le dogme de la fraternité commençait à lier ensemble les races et les nations diverses, mais seulement aux degrés correspondants de la hiérarchie féodale. Dans toute l'Europe, en effet, les héritiers des conquérants, les Nobles, se saluaient comme égaux, foulant aux pieds les manants et les roturiers, qui n'étaient point à leurs yeux des hommes de leur espèce. Mais ceux-ci, partout asservis, s'appelaient frères entre eux, et pressentant même dans l'avenir le Règne de Dieu et de sa justice, comprenaient déjà que leurs oppresseurs n'étaient que leurs frères aînés dans la grande famille humaine.

L'esprit et le droit des temps féodaux étaient l'esprit aristocratique et le droit nobiliaire. L'un et l'autre, quoique considérablement altérés et affaiblis par les grands progrès sociaux des derniers-siècles, subsistaient encore en France, lorsque la révolution de 89 y vint clore l'ancien Régime et inaugurer l'Ordre nouveau.

§ II.

L'ordre nouveau ou chrétien et démocratique.

L'Ordre Nouveau s'est dégagé de l'Ordre Féodal par les développements de l'industrie, des sciences, du Travail, par les lentes mais irrésistibles conquêtes de l'intelligence sur la force, du génie de la création sur le génie de la guerre. Le droit des Sociétés modernes est le droit commun; leur principe, le principe chrétien de l'unité spécifique des races dans l'humanité, d'où est sorti le principe politique de l'égalité du droit des citoyens dans l'Etat. Leur esprit est l'esprit *démocratique*.

L'Epoque de 89 a donc marqué dans l'histoire de l'humanité la grande séparation entre l'Ordre ancien et l'Ordre nouveau; entre le droit de la force et le droit du travail, entre le droit aristocratique, le droit de la conquête perpétué par la naissance, et le droit commun, le droit de Tous à Tout, LE DROIT DÉMOCRATIQUE.

Page 2. See p. 48 in this edition.

8

La Civilisation, qui a commencé par la Féodalité nobiliaire, *et dont le développement a affranchi les industrieux
des servitudes* personnelles ou directes, *aboutit donc aujour-
d'hui à la* Féodalité industrielle, *qui opère les servitudes*
collectives ou indirectes *des travailleurs.*

§ VI.

Misère croissante des travailleurs par la *dépréciation du salaire ;*
effet de la *libre concurrence.*

Ce qui est vrai, de grande classe à grande classe, de la
classe des prolétaires dénués de tout à celle des possesseurs
du fonds et des instruments de travail, est également vrai des
forts aux faibles dans chaque classe.

Ainsi la libre concurrence de prolétaires à prolétaires, les
nécessités de l'existence qui contraignent ceux-ci à trouver
chaque matin, aux conditions même les plus dures, du travail
et *un maître,* les conduisent forcément à mettre leurs bras au
rabais. De telle sorte que, quand les travailleurs abondent, et
c'est le cas général, la libre concurrence entre ces malheureux
les poussant à offrir leurs bras au plus bas prix possible, le
taux de la journée tend à tomber partout à la dernière li-
mite des nécessités extrêmes de l'existence : ce qui aggrave
surtout la position du prolétaire chargé de famille. La concurrence des maîtres entre eux force d'ailleurs chacun de
ceux-ci, *quelle que puisse être son humanité,* à n'accorder que
les salaires les plus exigus; car un chef de maison ne saurait,
sans courir à une perte certaine, payer à ses ouvriers des
salaires plus élevés que ses concurrents. — Ainsi, le Mécanisme odieux de la libre concurrence sans garanties, brise
toutes les lois de la justice et de l'humanité. Il suffit que le
salaire des ouvriers dans une branche tombe sur un seul point
pour que les maîtres soient forcément conduits à imposer
bientôt la même diminution sur tous les autres points dans la
même branche. Le salaire décroissant, les prix décroissent,
se nivellent ; et les maîtres se retrouvent bientôt dans les
mêmes conditions réciproques , sans faire plus de bénéfice
qu'auparavant. Seulement le sort des masses a empiré...

Sample skips to page 8. See p. 53 in this edition.

9

La libre concurrence, c'est-à-dire la concurrence anarchique et sans organisation, a donc cet inhumain, cet exécrable caractère, qu'elle est partout et toujours *dépréciative du salaire*. — Après avoir plongé les classes ouvrières en masse dans le gouffre de la misère, elle les y enfonce sous un poids toujours plus lourd! — En Irlande, en Angleterre, en Belgique, en France, partout où règne la libre concurrence, où rien n'arrête l'essor désordonné d'un industrialisme sans frein, le sort des classes ouvrières devient nécessairement plus misérable et plus abject; et ce n'est pas seulement contre elles-mêmes que ces classes ont à lutter, c'est contre des machines qui ne dépensent plus que quelques centimes par force d'homme!

§ VII.

Réduction des classes moyennes; dangers qui les menacent par la suprématie de l'aristocratie d'argent.

Ce n'est pas tout: des phénomènes analogues se passent dans la classe des possesseurs du fond et des instruments de travail. Les forts y dominent tout aussi fatalement, y égorgent tout aussi impitoyablement les faibles. Et si les premiers résultats de cette lutte à conditions aussi monstrueusement inégales, qu'on décore du nom de liberté industrielle, est la réduction immédiate des masses prolétaires en Servage collectif; le second résultat, tout aussi forcé que le précédent, c'est l'écrasement progressif de la petite et de la moyenne propriété, de la petite et de la moyenne industrie, du petit et du moyen commerce, sous le poids de la grande propriété, sous les roues colossales de la grande industrie et du grand commerce.

Dans quelque branche que ce soit, en effet, les grands capitaux, les grandes entreprises font la loi aux petites. La vapeur, les machines, les grandes manufactures, ont eu facilement raison, partout où elles se sont présentées, des petits et des moyens ateliers. A leur approche les anciens métiers et les artisans ont disparu pour ne plus laisser que des fabriques et des prolétaires. De plus, on voit surgir, presque à chaque

4*

Page 9. See p. 54 in this edition.

10

instant, une découverte inattendue, qui, renouvelant brusquement toute une branche de la production, porte la perturbation dans les établissements. Après avoir cassé les bras des ouvriers, jeté sur le pavé des masses d'hommes remplacés tout-à-coup par des machines, elle écrase les maîtres à leur tour. D'un bout de la France à l'autre, d'ailleurs, la petite et la moyenne propriété agricole, grévées d'hypothèques ruineuses, dévorées par l'usure, gémissent sous l'oppression du Capital qui les exploite toutes deux et pompe, au moyen du prêt, de la manière la plus commode et sans se donner aucun soin d'exploitation ni de fermage, le plus clair des revenus que le dur travail de vingt-cinq millions de laboureurs tire annuellement du sol,

Enfin, qui résiste aux crises, qui en profite, qui rachète à vil prix les établissements péniblement créés par de longs efforts? qui gagne par la disette comme par l'abondance? qui fait de magnifiques coups de filets dans les plus grands désastres? qui s'empare de toutes les positions, de toutes les lignes stratégiques, de toutes les bases d'opération du commerce et de l'industrie? Qui envahit tout, qui devient maître de tout, sinon la haute spéculation, la haute banque, et, en toute branche, les gros Capitaux?

Oui, il est temps pour les classes moyennes, déjà fort entamées, d'y prendre garde. L'Argent envahit tout; la puissance des gros Capitaux s'accroît incessamment : ils attirent et absorbent, dans tous les ordres, les petits capitaux et les moyennes fortunes.

§ VIII.

Division de la société en deux classes : un petit nombre possédant tout, le grand nombre dépouillé de tout.

Ainsi, malgré le principe abstractivement démocratique de la liberté industrielle, ou plutôt par l'effet de cette liberté, *fausse et illusoire* comme toute liberté simple et non organisée, les capitaux gravitant sans contrepoids sur les capitaux, proportionnellement aux masses, viennent se concentrer dans les mains des plus forts détenteurs; et la Société tend à

Page 10. See p. 55 in this edition.

11

se diviser de plus en plus distinctement en deux grandes classes : Un petit nombre possédant tout ou presque tout, maître absolu de tout dans le domaine de la propriété, du commerce et de l'industrie ; et le grand nombre ne possédant rien, vivant dans une dépendance collective absolue des détenteurs du capital et des instruments de travail, obligé de louer pour un salaire précaire et toujours décroissant, ses bras, ses talents et ses forces aux Seigneurs Féodaux de la Société moderne.

Ce tableau de l'état social actuel, cette description du mouvement qui nous emporte rapidement vers la constitution régulière de la Féodalité nouvelle, n'a plus rien de prophétique. C'est de l'histoire contemporaine. Que l'on ergote, si l'on veut, sur tel ou tel terme d'une exposition générale et nécessairement sommaire : il n'en reste pas moins vrai que la Société marche à grands pas à la constitution d'une Aristocratie aussi lourde qu'ignoble ; que nous y sommes, que nous l'avons atteinte ; qu'elle nous enlace et nous serre ; qu'elle pèse sur le peuple, et qu'elle dompte, réduit et asservit chaque jour, individu par individu et commerce par commerce, les classes intermédiaires elles-mêmes.

Et ce phénomène n'est pas particulier à la France : c'est un phénomène social qui caractérise la Civilisation moderne. Il se développe avec d'autant plus d'énergie dans chaque État que l'industrialisme civilisé y atteint un degré plus avancé. Il suit pas à pas la marche du système commercial, manufacturier, et l'invasion des machines. Notre industrialisme à libre concurrence est un Mécanisme colossal d'une énorme puissance, qui pompe incessamment les richesses nationales pour les concentrer dans les grands réservoirs de l'Aristocratie nouvelle, et qui fabrique des légions faméliques de pauvres et de prolétaires. La Grande-Bretagne présente au plus haut degré ce phénomène de la concentration des capitaux entre les mains d'une Aristocratie peu nombreuse, de l'amoindrissement des classes moyennes, de la quasi-annihilation politique et sociale de la Bourgeoisie, d'un Prolétariat et d'un Paupérisme envahissants. La France et la Belgique, les deux pays qui suivent de plus près l'Angleterre dans la voie de ce faux industrialisme, sont aussi les pays où s'organise le plus rapidement la Féodalité nouvelle.

Page 11. See p. 56 in this edition.

22

§ IV.

Accroissement énorme de la 'richesse sociale par l'Association.

Le Capital, le Travail et le Talent sont les trois éléments de la production, les trois sources de la richesse, les trois rouages du mécanisme industriel, les trois grands moyens primitifs du développement social. Supposez par la pensée l'atelier social organisé sur la base de l'Association, les trois éléments de la production savamment combinés dans l'économie industrielle, les trois rouages du mécanisme harmonieusement engrenés. A la lutte anarchique d'une concurrence aveugle, à la guerre des capitaux contre les capitaux, du travail contre le capital, des industries contre les industries ; au désordre général, au choc de toutes les forces productives, à la déperdition des valeurs engagées dans mille mouvements contraires, se substituent la plus puissante combinaison productive, l'aménagement et l'utile emploi de toutes les forces ! La richesse, coulant à pleins bords des sources élargies et multipliées de la Production, se distribue régulièrement et hiérarchiquement au sein des populations, arrose et fertilise toutes les parties du sol national. Le Travail prend sa part légitime de l'accroissement des richesses en proportion de son concours ; les classes dénuées et faméliques s'élèvent à l'aisance ; les prolétaires deviennent consommateurs et ouvrent à la production de grands [marchés intérieurs dont les demandes s'accroissent sans cesse.

§ V.

Cercle vicieux ; rapport des salaires et des débouchés ; engorgement de l'industrie par la misère des travailleurs.

Les nations industrieuses cherchent à grands efforts des débouchés extérieurs à leurs fabrications. L'Angleterre, tourmentée d'une pléthore sous laquelle elle respire à peine, fait

Sample skips to page 22. See p. 65 in this edition.

23

des efforts surhumains pour verser le trop-plein de ses fabriques sur toutes les plages. Elle s'ouvre à coups de canon les portes du vieil empire de la Chine. Elle parcourt incessamment et à main armée le globe, demandant partout des consommateurs... et, à côté d'elle en Irlande, et dans son propre sein depuis la Cornouailles jusqu'au Sutherland, et dans ses immenses possessions de l'ancien et du nouveau monde, d'innombrables masses de travailleurs dépérissent et meurent ou se révoltent, parce que les absurdes rigueurs du régime de la concurrence ne leur permettent pas de consommer le plus strict nécessaire !

Quoi ! les nations les plus civilisées s'affaissent sous le poids mortel d'une production trop abondante ; et dans leur sein même les légions ouvrières s'étiolent faute de pouvoir, par les conditions du salaire, participer à la consommation de cette production exubérante ! N'est-il pas aussi absurde qu'inhumain, ce régime industriel qui menace ruine *faute de consommateurs*, et qui rétribue si misérablement le Travail, qu'il obstrue et se ferme à lui-même, sur tous les marchés, les canaux les plus larges de la consommation ?

Poussez ce cruel et stupide système aux conséquences extrêmes vers lesquelles il tend : supposez que cet industrialisme parvienne à remplacer, en toutes fonctions, le bras de l'homme par les machines, et, de réductions en réductions, arrive à l'anéantissement des salaires ! vous réalisez l'idéal des économistes, la production au *plus bas prix possible*, et en même temps la victoire absolue du Capital sur le Travail. Mais que deviennent vos immenses produits ? où se placent-ils ? qui les consomme ? et si les populations consentent à mourir de faim paisiblement et légalement, en respectant ce que vous appelez l'ordre et le droit sacré de la propriété, ne verrez-vous pas votre mécanisme producteur crouler sur lui-même et vous écraser sous ses ruines ?

Que si au contraire vous supposez une organisation de l'industrie rationnelle, équitable, chrétienne ; qui rétribue le travail avec charité, avec justice, avec libéralité ; qui tienne compte des droits du Travail aussi sacrés pour le moins que ceux de la Propriété ; qui donne au Travail et au Talent comme au Capital la part qui leur revient légitimement dans l'œuvre de la Production des richesses ; ne voyez-vous pas que l'aisance et le bien-être se répandant dans toutes les

Page 23. See p. 66 in this edition.

24

classes : que vos grands marchés nationaux qui s'obstruaient, s'élargissent ; que vos débouchés qui diminuaient, s'agrandissent ; et que les bénéfices légitimes du Capital s'accroissent incessamment par cela même que ceux du Travail et du Talent augmentent dans une proportion correspondante ?

§ VI.

Intérêt commun des trois classes.

IL n'y a donc pas, constatons-le, d'antinomie radicale dans la nature des choses ; il n'y a pas de contradiction et de guerre nécessaire entre les principes et les éléments de la Próduction. Les luttes acharnées des capitaux contre les capitaux , du capital contre le travail et contre le talent, des industries entre elles, des maîtres contre les ouvriers, des ouvriers contre les maîtres, de chacun contre tous et de tous contre chacun, ne sont point des conditions fatalement attachées à la vie de l'humanité. Elles ne tiennent qu'au Mécanisme actuel de l'industrie, au système de la Concurrence anarchique et désordonnée, de cette liberté sans organisation que nous ont vantés, avec un si triste succès, les écoles fondées par les économistes de l'Angleterre. Il est évidemment possible d'accroître considérablement la richesse publique par une sage organisation de l'atelier social, par une application progressive du principe de l'Association, et de rétribuer abondamment le travail des masses, sans rien prendre à ceux qui possèdent.

Qu'on ne parle donc plus de la liberté industrielle , telle qu'elle a été comprise et réalisée de nos jours ; sinon pour la condamner et la maudire ! Qu'on ne parle plus de l'antagonisme fondamental du travail et du talent , sinon pour constater que cet antagonisme résulte d'un mécanisme funeste sous tous les points de vue : funeste au développement de la production par le resserrement de la consommation ; funeste aux classes supérieures par les crises et les réactions désastreuses qu'il provoquerait sans aucun doute ; funeste aux classes inférieures enfin, par les misères croissantes dont il les accable et qui jetteraient forcément ces classes dans la

Page 24. See p. 67 in this edition.

MANIFESTO OF DEMOCRACY

Part One

THE STATE OF SOCIETY

I. Of the Interests and Needs of Society

§ I.

The Ancient and Feudal Social Orders

Ancient societies had as their basic principle, Might makes right; their politics was War; their goal was Conquest; and their economic system was Slavery, which is the most total, inhumane, and barbarous form of man's exploitation by man. Free men, rich or poor, made war and consumed: the slave was the producer. SLAVERY was the base of society; its summit was WAR. Human compassion didn't extend any further than a Nation's borders. Foreign policy consisted of one Nation's merciless domination over others; domestic policy was slavery and the spirit of caste. Such was the nature of the ancient social order.

The feudal order, derived from conquest, was merely conquest legitimated. Its major feature was still war, and, above all, the permanent institutional sanction it gave to the *de facto* privileges of conquest.

Its economic system was a slightly less harsh and brutal form of man's exploitation by man, Serfdom. Human compassion, unfolding in the radiant warmth of early Christianity, was reaching beyond the narrow boundaries of the Nation. The principle of fraternity began to bind together diverse peoples and nations, but the bonds corresponded to the feudal hierarchy. In all Europe the progeny of the conquerors, the Nobility, recognized each other as equals, trampling underfoot the peasant and commoners who in their view weren't even men of the same species. But these people, everywhere subjugated, were treating each other as brothers and were even prefiguring the advent of God's Kingdom and its justice. They already understood that their oppressors were merely their elder brothers in the great human family.

The spirit and the rights of feudal times were the aristocratic spirit and the rights of nobles. Both, however much changed or weakened by the great social progress of the last few centuries, still prevailed in France until the revolution of 1789 ended the *Ancien Régime* and inaugurated the new Order.

§ II.

The New Order: Christian and Democratic

The NEW ORDER arose out of the Feudal Order through developments in industry, science, and labor, and by the slow but irresistible gains of intelligence over brute force, the creative genius over the military genius. Right is universal in modern Societies, and their basic principle is the Christian concept joining all members of the human species. From this comes the political principle of equal rights for all citizens. The spirit of these Societies is *democratic.*

The epoch of 1789 thus marks the great division in humanity's history between the old Order and the new Order, between right based on might and right based on work, between the aristocratic right, the right of conquest perpetuated by birth, and universal right, the right of All to All, THE DEMOCRATIC RIGHT.

§ III.

Separation of the democratic and revolutionary principles

The new democratic right has since 1789 been sanctioned by the first article of all our constitutions: "All Frenchmen are equal before the law, and in public offices and duties."

Because this new democratic right came into the world by a

revolution, was proclaimed, established and defended by a revolution, and owed its success to the success of a revolution, it isn't surprising that the democratic principle has long been associated with the revolutionary principle.

The democratic right could have been incorporated into Society through progressive organizational reforms that would have completed peacefully, across the board, the gradual transformation of the old feudal Society that was already well underway.

But the natural movement of synthesis and inclusion that could have provided an orderly transformation of the old Society hadn't been promoted and directed intelligently by the successors of Henry IV, Richelieu, and Louis XIV; as the new spirit hadn't been wisely and closely monitored during its powerful expansion, the result was an explosion. The *ancien régime* was violently overthrown, and on its fragments the two principles of right clashed in the most hostile confrontation, creating an explosion long reverberating on European soil, and starting a war whose outcome was already decided by the eternal laws governing the world. When it is time for the past to be transformed, if the past resists the inevitable it will perish in violence.

The course of events thus drove the modernizing movement onto the path of violent Protest, of Revolution, and War. Consequently, War, Revolution, and violent Protest have long been the leading manifestations of the new spirit. Instead of implanting its principles of liberty and justice into social organization, the new spirit is almost entirely preoccupied with the struggle against the past. In this regard, the generations that ended the 18th century and those that began the 19th believed fervently that since the Revolution had ended, the War had ceased, the privileges of birth had been abolished, and the principle of equality had been victoriously inscribed in the law, the new structure would be achieved in actuality and the new Order founded and established.

It was a serious mistake.

All the work of organizing the New Order remains to be done.

This work is the problem and task of our era; it is the puzzle that Destiny's spirit charges us to resolve.

§ IV.

The revolutionary work is done; the democratic work is hardly begun

Revolution, from 1789 to 1830, has shown only the negative and abstract side of the new democratic right. It has overthrown the last vestiges of the Feudal Order based on war and the privileges of a hereditary nobility; it has inscribed the democratic principle of citizen equality at the head of the law. It has even, we must recognize, created a representative system in the political order, which, insofar as it is based on elections without regard to inherited status is the defining political institution of modern Society. It has also tried to make elementary education more accessible through a new primary school system. But it has left the entire economic order without organization, direction, or any regulation. It has abolished the guild wardens, privileges, and traditional corporations that represented illiberal economic organization, but it hasn't replaced them with a better organization. It has abandoned the whole social and economic arena, the entire domain of Production and the Distribution of wealth, to the most unbridled *laissez-faire*, the most anarchic competition, the blindest war of all against all, and consequently, to Monopoly by the largest enterprises.

Now a person's status in the economic, social, and political orders is based only on *money, education,* or *connections.* Education and connections presuppose leisure or wealth. Without a fair organization of work, wealth is generally transmitted only by birth and alliances. The result is that, despite the philosophical liberalism of democratic rights, the legal destruction of former aristocratic rights, the constitutional equality of citizens before the law and in official capacities, and the abolition of royal franchises, the current social Order remains an aristocratic Order, no longer, it is true, *in theory and law,* but *in fact.*

Also, despite individual exceptions that don't disprove the general rule, in today's society those who are born into penury, poverty, or misery live out their lives in penury, poverty, or misery, and they transmit this fatal inheritance to their descendants, who, destined to remain like them in penury, poverty, or misery, indeed remain there.

It is also true that the wealthy and comfortable classes reproduce the wealthy and comfortable social strata of the following generations. Except that, thanks to bad luck in the current anarchic economy, to the miserable struggles resulting from free competition without limits or rules, and to the increasing domination of big Capitalists, unfortunately a large number of individuals and families in the comfortable class, sometimes even those of the wealthy class, are at risk of falling and do fall into poverty.

Thus, although the new democratic right no longer recognizes any natural disqualifications of persons or classes—on the contrary, it proclaims very democratically the equal social and political capacity of everyone to everything—nevertheless, top and middling positions in politics, industry, finance, and commerce, and nearly all public offices and liberal professions are monopolized *in fact* by upper and middle class families that hold onto them and transmit them among themselves, while the menial jobs, the hard work, and the painful, thankless, repugnant, risky, and miserably paid tasks, remain the permanent lot of lower class families.

It is therefore correct to argue that except for very few individuals who make their way out of the lower classes by means of quite exceptional circumstances or aptitudes enabling them to ascend the social ladder, and except for a rather larger number from the comfortable or wealthy classes who are thrown into poverty or misery by social and economic crises, the upper and lower *classes* are perpetuated by birth.

If that is really true, it is obvious that our social condition, which is *democratic in theory and in law*, is still, as we are saying, *aristocratic in fact*. Constitutionally, legally, and abstractly, there are no longer castes in the nation. Practically, precisely, and realistically, we still live in a regime of castes. Only it is no longer law, rights, or political principle that create barriers between the major divisions of the French people, but our *economic and social organization*.

§ V.

Rapid development of a new Feudalism through anarchic free competition – Collective Serfdom of workers

Today the gravest phenomenon is becoming clearly evident, even to those who are least observant. This phenomenon is the rapid and powerful development of a NEW FEUDALISM, an *industrial and financial* Feudalism, which is steadily replacing the noble and military Aristocracy of the *ancien Régime* by annihilating or impoverishing the middle classes.

After the great explosion of 1789, the destruction of the former political Order, and the abrogation of feudal property and the guild system, *economic liberty* was proclaimed, and Society believed it was forever rid of any exclusive ruling Aristocracy.

In assuming this, they have reckoned badly. The evidence is plain, and the reason, furthermore, is easy to grasp—here it is:

Once the great agitation subsided, the new situation assumed, and society returned to normalcy, in the social and economic arenas there remained only individuals confronting each other, left in *complete freedom* for themselves and their own resources. But some were equipped with capital, talents, and education, and occupied powerful, high positions; others, the members of the most numerous classes, had neither capital, education, nor prior training to develop their talents. They stagnated, relegated to the lowest rungs of the social ladder.

What can result in such a state of things, from this economic freedom on which so much is staked, from this famous principle of *free competition* that is so fervently believed to be the defining characteristic of democratic organization? Nothing can come of it except general servitude to the wealthy, well-armed class, a collective feudal subjugation for the masses deprived of capital, instruments of production, education, and economic strongholds.

"The lists are open; all individuals are called to the tournament; the conditions are the same for all combatants." Indeed! Only one thing is forgotten: on this great battlefield, some are educated, combat-trained, equipped, and armed to the teeth; they have a huge supply of provisions, supplies, ammunition, and weapons; and they hold the high ground. Others, deprived, stripped, uneducated, and starved, must beg from their very adversaries for any available work at a meager wage just to live from day to day and support their wives and children.

Absolute liberty, without organization, is then nothing but the *absolute abandonment* of the disarmed and deprived masses to the mercy of the armed and equipped forces.

Civilization, which began with the FEUDALISM OF NOBLES, *gradually freed the industrious from* personal or direct servitude. *Today it has evolved into* INDUSTRIAL FEUDALISM, *which imposes on workers* collective or indirect *servitude.*

§ VI.

Increasing misery of workers due to falling wages; effect of *free competition*

The relationship between the classes, the wealthy class that possesses capital and the instruments of production and the proletarian class that is stripped of everything, also holds true between the strong and weak of each class.

Thus, there is free competition among proletarians. Survival needs that force them each day under the most difficult conditions to find work and *an employer* compel them to sell their labor at the lowest price. The result is that when workers are plentiful, and that is generally the case, free competition among these unfortunates forces them to offer their labor at the lowest possible price, and the day's wage falls everywhere to the cost of the barest necessities for survival, which is especially hard on those proletarians supporting a family. The competition among employers forces each of them, *despite benevolent intentions,* to pay only the most pitiful wages, because a capitalist knows that he risks failure by paying his workers wages higher than those of his competitors. Thus, the odious Engine of free competition without safeguards breaks all the laws of justice and humanity. When workers' wages fall in one job within an industrial division, employers are soon forced to impose the same cut on all the other jobs in that division. Wages and prices decrease in a downward spiral, and the employers quickly find themselves in the same reciprocating situation, without doing any better than formerly. Only the situation of the masses has become worse.

Free competition, that is, anarchic, unregulated competition, has this inhumane, reprehensible nature: it always lowers wages everywhere. After having plunged the working classes into the gulf of misery, it keeps them there under an increasingly heavy weight! In Ireland, England, Belgium, France, wherever free competition reigns, nothing halts the mounting disorder of unchecked industrialism. The situation of the working classes necessarily becomes more miserable and abject. Furthermore, it isn't only against each other that these classes must struggle, but also against machines that provide manpower for only a few pennies!

§ VII.

Reduction of the middle classes; dangers facing them from the dominant moneyed aristocracy

That isn't all: analogous phenomena occur in the class possessing capital and the instruments of production. There as well the strong inevitably dominate all, and with no regrets ruin the weak. And if the first consequence of this struggle on monstrously unequal terms is the sudden reduction of the proletarian masses into collective Serfdom, the second consequence, just as inevitable as the first, is the progressive crushing of small and middle-sized property, industry, and business under the weight of the wealthy owners, under the colossal wheels of big business and industry.

In every branch of the economy, the big capitals and large enterprises make the law for the small. Steam engines, machinery, and large factories have always easily predominated wherever they have confronted small and middle-size workshops. At their approach, the old trades and artisans disappeared, leaving only factories and proletarians. Furthermore, again and again some unexpected invention appears, which renovates an entire branch of production, and sends fear through the entire industry. After having broken the workers' arms and thrown into the gutter all those men suddenly replaced by machines, it crushes the employers in their turn. In addition, from one end of France to the other, small and middle-sized farms, burdened with ruinous mortgages and consumed by usury, groan under the oppression of Capital. Exploitative loans and excessive rents suck up the well-deserved returns that the hard work of 25 million workers draws annually from the soil.

Finally, who survives the crises, profits from them, and buys up for practically nothing businesses created with many years of hard work? Who gains from scarcity as well as from abundance? Who benefits magnificently from the greatest disasters? Who seizes all the favorable positions, strategic posts, and bases of operation in commerce and industry? Who invades all and becomes master of all, but the big speculators and banks, and, in every industry, the big Capitals?

Yes, it is time for the middle classes, already seriously encroached upon, to watch out. Money invades all; the power of the big Capitals relentlessly increases. They attract and absorb, in all domains, the small capitals and the middle-sized fortunes.

§ VIII.

Division of society into two classes: a small number owning everything, the many robbed of everything

Thus, despite the theoretically democratic principle of economic freedom, or rather, because of this freedom, which is *false and illusory* like all simple and unorganized freedoms, capitals press on other capitals without counterweight and in proportion to their mass, becoming concentrated in the hands of the largest holders. Society tends to be divided more and more sharply into two major classes: an elite owning all or nearly all, absolute master in the realms of landed property, commerce, and industry; and the masses owning nothing, living in total collective dependence on the owners of capital and instruments of production, and who, for a precarious and always decreasing wage, are forced to rent their arms, talents, and strength to the Feudal Lords of modern Society.

This picture of the current social situation, this description of developments quickly bringing us towards a veritable constitution of the new Feudalism is no longer prophetic. It is current history. One may quibble over the terminology of this general and necessarily brief exposition. It remains nevertheless true that Society is moving rapidly towards instituting an overbearing and vile Aristocracy. We are there; we have arrived at it. It ties and binds us; it weighs on the people; and it subjugates, grinds down, and enslaves, person by person, and business by business, the middle classes themselves.

And this phenomenon isn't unique to France. It is a social phenomenon characteristic of modern Civilization. It develops most forcefully in those Nations where industrialism has made the greatest advances. It follows step by step the progress of commerce, manufacturing, and the invasion of machinery. Our free competition economy is a colossal Machine of enormous power, which incessantly sucks up the national wealth to concentrate it in the great reservoirs of the new Aristocracy, and which fabricates starving legions of the poor and the proletariat. Great Britain exhibits this phenomenon to the greatest degree: the concentration of capital in the hands of a small Aristocracy, the shrinking of the middle classes, the nearly total political and social annihilation of the Bourgeoisie, and an increasing Proletariat and Pauperism. France and Belgium, the two countries that most closely follow England in this path of illusory industrialism, are also the countries where the new Feudalism is most rapidly emerging.

Finally, Germany, deeply frightened by the spectacle that England and France are presenting, now hesitates to stimulate its own material progress, which threatens such dire social consequences.

§ IX.

Bondage of the government to the new aristocracy

Do You Want to know to what extent this disastrous Feudalism is already rooted in the soil and dominant in political and social development? Let us put to one side the fact that a great monopolistic scheme was responsible for the Empire's fall, by causing a fatal six-week delay to the Russian campaign. Haven't we seen this very year the Government submitting to the dictates of the feudal canal Companies that facilitate the commerce of our richest provinces, setting and collecting at will the tolls on our lines of communication like the Lords of fortified manors in the counties and baronies during the Middle Ages, and all the while laughing at the useless protests of the central Government? Haven't we seen this same Government, while deploring this domination by the feudal Companies, shamefully agree that it was itself incapable of developing and directing railroads, to the profit of the great all-powerful Vassals of the Bank? Meanwhile, the small Belgian Government has in a few years covered its land with railroads, which we can see it administers very well and very democratically. Finally, to top it off, when the French King had a great idea and tried to create a Franco-Belgian union, didn't we see the two Governments, the two Nations, the two Kings, stopped by the insolent resistance of a few large industrial property owners? The two Governments, the two Nations, the two Kings, didn't they bend to the will of these all-powerful Vassals? Has it required more than a week to impose the paramount will of these new Lords on the presumed holders of national Sovereignty? With this example, isn't it evident that no longer do the King, the Ministers, and the Nation govern, but rather industrial and financial Feudalism?[i]

§ X.

The Social Revolutions

Don't be mistaken. Such a situation, if it continues and progresses, is full of danger. The French people will not let themselves be driven into the same corner where the urban and rural working people of Ireland and England have been dumped. The French Bourgeoisie will not allow themselves be fleeced and stripped of their property, deprived of their political influence, and tossed into the Proletariat. Universal Monopoly cannot, in our century, gravitate into the hands of an elite class without arousing furious hatred against that class. Already, among the

Chartists of England, where for obvious reasons feudalism is more advanced than here, these social hatreds, the precursors of revolutions in which property rights are at stake, have reached a frightful intensity. There would have been ten revolutions here before our working classes reached this stage of reaction and hate.

What will become of Civilization, what will become of Government, and what will become of the upper classes, if industrial Feudalism, extending itself through all of Europe, provokes the great cry of social war, "*To live working or to die fighting,*" and rouses the immense legions of Modern Slavery?

Well, if the wise ones in Government, the intelligent, liberal Bourgeoisie, and Scientists don't reflect on this, it is certain that the movement igniting European Societies will lead straight to social revolution, and that we will be on the road to a European-wide Jacquerie.*

On this matter some stubborn conservatives, fearful ex-liberal pigs, don't want to hear any discussion or prediction. They are angry that we haven't delicately spared them from the truths that might disturb the moronic slumber of these egoistic consumers. These former revolutionaries, now fat and satisfied, think it better to avoid mentioning the people's unhappiness, the miseries of slavery, the proletariat's hatred, and the parallel incursions of industrial Feudalism and Pauperism. This avoidance is supposed to spirit away any future trouble and sustain the illusion that all is for the best in the world where these gentlemen are prospering. "Preach to the workers," say these shortsighted, heartless men—all atheists, "the consolation of religion. It is true that they aren't as wealthy as we are, but it is impossible to improve their situation."

Well! With good reason, the working classes don't believe that they must forever be commodities with their prices rising or falling as if they were merely proletarian raw material in the marketplace. They want Society to guarantee them life and work; they are beginning to understand that the *right to Work* is a right no less sacred than the *right to Property.* Unfortunately, the

---

*Peasant uprising of 1358. [ed.]

great injustice victimizing them makes them unjust in turn, so that in the three most developed Nations—England, France, and Germany—they are beginning to question the right to Property and to reject it!

Who are today the true conservatives: the intelligent and foresighted ones, those who demand that the political and social Powers inform themselves about the current situation in order to remedy it by providing legitimate redress for unrecognized rights and interests, and thus permit Society to develop safely, or those who, satiated, content with their own lot, and lacking courage to probe the deep misery of society, believe that we mustn't think of such things, and consequently let a storm gather that could overthrow everything?

Since when does one cure serious illnesses by keeping them secret? Since when does one heal wounds and ulcers by covering them up, turning one's head, and refusing to examine or probe them?

§ XI.

The social hell. Absolute necessity for a solution

We are arguing here that our system of free competition, lauded by foolish political Economy and instituted to abolish monopolies, results only in the universal organization of large monopolies in every industry; that everywhere free competition depresses wages, that it accomplishes nothing but a permanent war of labor, machinery, and capital—all against all—a war where the weak are destined to perish; that it makes failures, bankruptcies, stoppages, and crises endemic in the economic system; that it unceasingly deposits debris and ruins throughout the land; and finally, that for their hard labor the lower and middle classes obtain only a troubled, miserable existence, always precarious, and full of anxiety and unhappiness.

We learn from the most authoritative documents,[ii] that while a small number of the wealthy become even richer, the situation of the industrious middle classes continually worsens. Our industrial system is therefore a veritable *Hell;* it enacts on an enormous scale the most brutal concepts of ancient myths. Our masses, naked and poor, are tossed into the waves of enormous luxury in great cities, where they see overflowing coffers in the currency and gold dealers' offices and shops filled with rich food and fine clothes of elegant fabrics. They then are splashed by the fancy carriages, and aroused by the sounds and songs coming from the theaters. Thus tormented by viewing all the pleasures denied to them, isn't this a gigantic human enactment of the anguish of Tantalus, tortured by eternal hunger and thirst in the midst of illusory fruits and water that forever evaded his desiccated mouth? Do you think that the agony of Sisyphus, fated to push a heavy rock to a mountain-top, which endlessly rolled right down again, is worse than that of unfortunate breadwinners who work steadily their whole lives to acquire a little wealth for their old age and their children, and who can hardly *make ends meet,* or of those who have painfully labored to create businesses only to lose them in the fire of raging competition or suddenly sink due to bankruptcy and the periodic crises of our economy? Finally, don't the fifty Danaides, forced to pour water ceaselessly into a bottomless vessel, accurately symbolize the abominable situation of the lower and middle classes, condemned to draw new torrents of wealth from the heart of the earth and the factories by relentless labor, which always flows through their hands and inevitably accumulates in the vast reservoirs of the moneyed Aristocracy?

Our economic system, based on competition with no guarantees or regulation, is thus nothing but a social Hell, a vast enactment of all the torments and miseries of ancient Tœnarus. There is however one difference: the victims of Tœnarus were the guilty, and in the mythological hell there were judges. . . .

And it is a similar state of things that is supposed to be accepted by contemporary intellectuals and the masses as normal organization, as the *nec plus ultra* of social institutions, as the best and fairest way to run industry and manage property! It is impossible! and we will not stop saying so until everybody recognizes this: attempting to immobilize Society in this system, trying to force Humanity to dead-end in this social Hell, will inevitably provoke frightful revolutions. Join us, therefore, intelligent and far-sighted Conservatives! Join us, enlightened men of the upper and middle classes, the men with heart in any class! Our Society, already scarred by fifty years of revolutions and heading quickly toward complete Feudalism, is in a crisis stage that calls for serious studies and prompt remedies if we wish to avoid an explosion!

It is obvious that our politicians, who don't bother themselves with organizational problems, as well as the entire antiquated political press, which is concerned only with parliamentary intrigues, ignore the major issue of our time and continue talking drivel. The problem of our time is above all social, economic, and industrial; and it is on the social terrain, where the great development of facts and ideas impassions our minds, that we must today direct our studies and produce knowledge and enlightenment.

II. The Two Solutions to the Social Problem

§ I.

The Community of Goods — Revolutionary principle or approach

Faced with this state of affairs, this difficult social question, two solutions, two ideas, two approaches can be and are being proposed.

One of these approaches is violent, destructive, revolutionary, and furthermore, illusory. It consists of attacking the very principle of private Property; denying that it is a right; despoiling, by force and law, the wealthy for the benefit of the poor and owners for the benefit of the proletarians; and finally, legislating the equality of conditions and the Community of goods.

Sparked by the rapid development of the Proletariat, Pauperism, and the new Feudalism, this idea ignited from the depths of a Society still smoldering with revolutionary fire. For some years it has been spreading among the working people, especially in the great industrial centers of France and England, and even in

Belgium, Switzerland, and Germany. It seduces and encourages the masses. It has on its side the huge advantage of great simplicity. *"No more property, no more owners! No more exploitation of man by man! No more inheritance! The earth for all!"* These formulas are very simple and understandable for the starving and oppressed masses, to whom they seem perfectly just so long as Society denies them the Right to Work, which is even more sacred than the Right to Property derived from it.

This essentially negative and revolutionary solution is but a limited, violent reaction (as are all the great reactions) against the social incursion and tyrannical domination of Capital. Communism will never arise where wealth and property are enjoying their legitimate rights and not exercising exclusive preponderance. These doctrines advocating the abolition of property are therefore protests against industrial Feudalism, protests tied to its progression, and will only increase in intensity until there is an explosion as capital's social – or rather its anti-social – pressure increases on the masses.

These phenomena are not simply philosophical speculations that can be lightly tossed aside or denied by the uninformed. They are facts about what is already happening. Chartism, Communism, and Saint-Simonian doctrines on the illegitimacy of inheritance are rapidly spreading throughout Europe.

§ II.

The Current Situation and 1789; Bourgeoisie and Proletarians

Towards the end of the *Ancien Régime* the Bourgeoisie was carried away by a great current of roiling philosophical and political ideas, quite incompatible with that regime and its privileges. The Nobility took little notice or laughed at them; bourgeois political and social ideas weren't serious matters. They were still dancing merrily at Louis XVI's court the night before the taking of the Bastille. Today, the doctrinaire Aristocracy that governs us, more self–satisfied and self-righteous, more *disdainful of the people*, their ideas, and their rights than was the old

French Nobility, is unaware of the dangerous ideas and doctrines developing in the proletarian strata lying beneath its gaze.* This serious movement remains a complete stranger to our Aristocracy. As for our four hundred deputies, there are probably not more than twenty who know that today the People read more than the financial Aristocracy, and what they read by the hundreds of thousands are books, leaflets, and pamphlets in which all aspects of the most serious and shocking social questions are discussed.

There is perfect parity between the two situations and the two epochs: the same disdain for the most urgent questions, ignorance of the powerful agitation going on below, and blindness! Happily, there are many in the ranks of the Bourgeoisie, and the intellectuals are beginning to wake up. The idea that we must find a remedy for the working class's material and spiritual miseries has seen the light of day. The bourgeois classes are revealing warm charitable impulses, and also are beginning to see that they, as well as the proletariat, have an interest in introducing guarantees into the economic order and resisting the financial Aristocracy's incursions. The opposition now appearing on the Chamber of Deputies' benches to this Aristocracy's high and mighty canal and railroad Companies indicates a salutary awakening among the representatives of the French Bourgeoisie. Will enlightenment arrive soon enough?

§ III.

Voluntary association: — the peaceful principle or method

We have said that there are only two possible ways of escaping from this new Feudal constitution. The first is equal distribu-

---

*The Doctrinaires were a political faction (there weren't formal political parties at that time) led by François Guizot and identified with the *juste milieu*, a compromise between absolutism and democracy. They supported the constitutional "July Monarchy" of the Orleanist, Louis Philippe, and an electorate limited to the upper bourgeoisie. The "Resistance" was another of their epithets, as they hoped to hold the line against any further democratization and had no plans for any substantial social or economic reforms. [ed.]

tion or the community of goods, a method completely negative and revolutionary, inherently anti-social, and also illusory. Such ideas we will challenge wherever and whenever they occur. Happily, this isn't the only option.

We have shown that Capital and Labor are in open war. The system of production, distribution, and division of wealth is nothing but an eternal battlefield. Controlling the instruments of Production, Capital consequently dictates the law to Labor. Furthermore, capitals struggle among each other; the big ones crush and absorb the small. The big capitals, concentrated in aristocratic families and multiplying their power through the system of huge joint stock Companies, are becoming more and more dominant. This preponderance keeps increasing, while the masses in a free enterprise system are unable to resist it, and thus it will inevitably sooner or later provoke a social revolutionary struggle. The classes that are always totally defeated in the economic arena will sooner or later appeal from a mock liberty and equality to a brutally effective equality—a redistribution of wealth. And when a revolution for redistribution is launched, the victors don't share the wealth; they blow off the defeated and take all. That is what the Bourgeoisie has done to the old Nobility and the Clergy.

Now, since the consequences of the war between Labor and Capital on the battleground of free competition inevitably results in either the crushing of labor and the small and middle sized capitals by the feudal capitals, or the crushing of property and capital by the workers' insurrection, there is only one way to dispel these two inevitable consequences of the struggle: IT IS TO THE END THE STRUGGLE. And if as is generally the case, peace is much more favorable to the respective interests of the belligerent parties than the war's prolonging would be even to the victors, it is evident that we must quickly find those conditions of peace that might obtain the conflicting parties' common consent.

There is a principle that has the power to convert economic competition into accord, divergence into convergence, and struggle into cooperation. It is ASSOCIATION.

When two rival enterprises create a single one with a *partnership agreement*, or when rival capitals unite in a great joint stock Company, these are hostile interests signing a peace treaty and henceforth developing cooperatively. But why stop at the Association of capitals? Why not ask that this principle of accord, unity, and harmony extend to the accord, unity, and harmony of Capital and Labor? Why not research and ascertain the practical conditions for agreement between Capital and Labor throughout the entire economy?

§ IV.

Enormous increase of social wealth through Association

Capital, Labor, and Talent are the three elements of production, the three sources of wealth, the three wheels of the industrial machine, and the three great basic resources of social development. Imagine the social system organized on the basis of Association, the three elements of production wisely combined in industry and the three wheels of the machine harmoniously in gear. Then the anarchic struggle of blind competition, the war of capitals against capitals, of labor against capital, of industries against each other, the general disorder, the collision of all productive forces, and the waste of resources invested in thousands of conflicting projects are replaced by the most powerful productive institution, and all resources efficiently managed! Wealth flowing copiously from the expanded Productive resources, distributed to the people on the basis of proportionality, waters and fertilizes the entire national soil. Labor receives its legitimate part in the increase of wealth proportionate to its cooperation; the destitute and starving classes become well-off; and the proletarians become consumers, creating a huge internal market for products, for which demand endlessly increases.

§ V.

Vicious circle; relationship of wages and markets; stoppage of industry by workers' poverty

Industrial nations frantically search for foreign outlets for their products. England, glutted with overproduction, makes superhuman efforts to dump its surplus manufactures onto every shore. With cannon shot, it opens the gates of the old Chinese empire. Heavily armed, it endlessly cruises the globe, seeking consumers everywhere . . . and yet, next door in Ireland, in the heart of its own country from Cornwall to Sutherland, and in its enormous possessions in the old and new worlds, innumerable masses of workers waste away and die, or they revolt because in this absurd free competition system they can't afford to consume even the basics for survival!

What! the most developed nations are sinking under the deadly weight of overproduction, while in their midst legions of workers are wasting away because their low wages prevent them from consuming this overwhelming production! Isn't it as absurd as it is inhumane, this economic system that may very well fail for want of buyers, and which pays Labor so poorly that it shuts out of its markets the largest group of potential consumers?

Extend this cruel, stupid system to the extreme toward which it is heading. Suppose that industrialism succeeds in replacing every type of human labor by machines, and to push the argument to its limit, wages decline to zero! You then achieve the economist's ideal, production at the lowest possible cost, and at the same time, the absolute triumph of Capital over Labor. But what will happen to your huge output of products? Where will they go? Who will consume them? If the people go willingly, peacefully, and legally to die of hunger, remaining respectful to your notions of order and the sacred right of property, won't you see your production system collapse on itself and crush you in the ruins?

What if, instead, you posit a rational, equitable, Christian industrial organization that rewards work with charity, justice, and liberality; holds Labor's rights to be at least as sacred as those of Property; and gives to Labor and Talent, as to Capital, their legitimate shares of the returns from wealth Production. Don't you see comfort and well-being spreading though all classes, your great, stopped-up, national markets expanding, your shrinking outlets growing, the legitimate rewards of Capital increasing incessantly, and those of Labor and Talent rising in corresponding proportion?

§ VI.

Common interest of the three classes

There isn't, we are arguing, any radical antinomy in the nature of things; there is no necessary contradiction or war between the principles and the elements of Production. The desperate struggles of capitals against capitals, of capital against labor and talent, of industries among themselves, of bosses against workers, of workers against bosses, of each against all and of all against each, are not inevitable conditions of human existence. They hold only for the current economic Apparatus, the system of anarchic, unregulated competition, and this freedom devoid of organization that has been so highly recommended to us, unfortunately successfully, by the English economic school. It is certainly possible to enlarge public wealth considerably by organizing the social system intelligently and applying the principle of Association progressively, and to reward the labor of the masses generously without taking anything from the propertied.

Let's not speak any more about free enterprise as it has been understood in our time, except to condemn it and curse it! Let's stop talking about the fundamental antagonism between labor and talent, except to argue that this antagonism results from a system that is disastrous from every point of view: disastrous to the development of production by its restriction of consumption, disastrous to the upper classes because of repeated crises and the violent reactions that it will undoubtedly provoke, and disastrous, finally, to the lower classes, because of the increasing miseries it imposes on them, which will force them into the path of bloody insurrection! Let's talk no longer about abolishing property, equal distribution or the community of goods, smashing machinery, and rowdyism! Rather let us speak of organizing for workers' interests and rights; introducing order, justice, and true liberty into the economy in production, distribution, and the division of wealth; and joining the interests of propertied and proletariat, rank and file, and leaders. Let's talk of making machines work FOR *the capitalists* and FOR *the people* and no longer FOR *the capitalists* AGAINST *the people*! Finally, let us speak of organizing the Association of classes into national Unity, and the Association of nations into Humanity! Those are the sane paths of modern States and Societies. Those are the problems now worth the attention of all serious intellectuals, all minds open to enlightenment, and all those souls who still hold to the great principles—the noble sentiments of country, liberty, and Christian fraternity that impassioned our fathers.

Summary of part one

LET US SUMMARIZE what we have established

Right gradually replaces Force, Industry dethrones War, and contemporary minds already completely recognize in the abstract the principle of equality and the universality of rights: the democratic principle.

The new democratic right, the Christian right of human equality and unity announced to the world by the French Revolution and victoriously upheld by France against the feudal, barbaric, aristocratic right, is written at the summit of the law. It is a permanent victory.

Since the democratic right, the Christian right, the right of all, has been conceived and applied merely by proclaiming liberty and equality, it is completely illusory, and the economic war has replaced the military one.

The economic war, like the military one, has victors and vanquished. Industrial Feudalism has established itself, like military Feudalism, by the disastrous triumph and permanent supremacy of the strong over the weak. The Proletariat is the modern Serfdom. A new Aristocracy whose titles are banknotes and stocks weighs more and more heavily on the Bourgeoisie itself and already dominates the government.

Such a state of things opposed to all the rights of humanity, to all the principles of the contemporary social temper, cannot continue without inciting new revolutions, revolutions no longer political but now social and directed against property itself, with their cries: "*Live working or die fighting! The world to the workers!"*

There is only one way to forestall these new Revolutions: it is the serious recognition of the right to Work, and an economic Organization based on the triple Association of capital, labor, and talent.

That organization is the task of modern Democracy.

Part Two

THE STATE OF OPINION

Study of the Great Divisions of Modern Democracy

§ I.

Universality of the democratic spirit in France; the Legitimist Party democratizes

THE CURRENT SITUATION, the critical needs of our time, the
problems to resolve, and the peaceful organizational principle of
their solution being known, it will be easy for us to describe the
current temper, to show the nature and importance of the various
shades of democratic opinion, and to determine the place of the
trend that we represent.

Let us first and foremost take note of a fact: it is that our era,
as our constitution, is democratic. In other words, that the language of *Democracy* is today destined to represent the passions,
the principles, and the rights now universally accepted *in theory*,
for which our fathers triumphantly endured the horrors of the
first Revolution.

For some time, ever since tumultuous urban riots have ceased,
the most brutal manifestations of the revolutionaries have been
quelled, and the calm has allowed us to resume the serious study
of ideas, the word "Democracy" has recovered the great, universal, and comprehensive significance that it is destined to have as
the basic idea of the century.

The anti-democratic doctrine of the inequality of birth, the
dogma of legal privileges, and the spirit of the *Ancien Régime*
have now disappeared. The Legitimist Party itself, nowadays,
professes—sincerely, we believe—liberal and democratic principles.*

It rejects and condemns all the abuses and privileges of the *Ancien Régime.* A *Memorandum* published by the party's executive committee formally proclaimed these principles. And if the royalist Press doesn't entirely support this *Memorandum,* it isn't because it is too saturated with the liberal ideas of our century, endorsing universal rights, representative government, and equality of citizens within the Nation; and celebrating the demise of feudal and divine right. On the contrary, certain party spokesmen have strongly censured the *Memorandum* because they find it not democratic enough. The parties most attached to the past are futile; they are always of their epoch, and the great current of modern ideas carries them along despite themselves. If Henry V could return to the Tuileries, we would not need to fear for citizens' rights, public liberties, or representative government, which his government would further enlarge in responsibilities rather than try to restrain.

The heirs of the old feudal party of the Aristocratic nobility today accept the democratic spirit. That recognized, we are going to show that the great modern, democratic party, in its entirety, is divided into three factions, forming a regular series. Its three branches can be classified according to the following nomenclature:

Retrograde democracy – revolutionary opinion;
Immobilist democracy – doctrinaire opinion;
Progressive democracy – peaceful and organizational opinion

§ II.

Political questions and *social* questions

BUT first let us proceed to a definition of the meaning we must give to these two terms: *political* issues and *social* issues. If we didn't focus on this matter it would be impossible to under-

---

*The faction supporting the Bourbon line of royalty, rather than the currently reigning Orleanist. They did not object to a constitutional monarchy. [ed.]

stand anything about the current trends in the public mind, the changing composition of Opinion, and above all, the problems that are now crying out for solutions and that already deeply disturb contemporary intellectuals.

In a very broad and general sense, the word *Political* designates the regulation of all aspects in the life of Societies. On its side, the term social is more readily given this broad meaning. But according to the narrow sense in which these terms are used, the word *politics*, in the language of contemporary journalists, means nothing more than the facts about the relationship of people to government, and governments among themselves. The nature, institutions, constitution, and composition of Power and its system and behavior comprise the content of political questions.

Worn-out discussions and theories and the new intrigues that these continue to stir up among the old parties constitute the domain of what is called the *Old Politics*.

Social questions, when contrasted with political questions, include especially information about the status, nature, and economy of Society; the relations among the classes; the institutions of property and industry; and the progress of welfare, positive liberty, enlightenment, intellect, morality, and public virtue. In a word: the general relationships among people and among nations, independently of transitory institutions, and the current leadership and politics of their various governments.

§ III.

Triumph of the democratic principle in the political order. Collapse of the old politics

NOW it is the case that since 1789 the work of the modern spirit has been applied nearly exclusively to the narrow political arena. In the economic and social orders, as we have already shown, the Revolution has acted only negatively and abstractly. It has overthrown the masterships, guild wardens, privileged corporations, and the feudal property system; it has gotten rid of the nobility and the clergy; but it hasn't created any new institutions.

It has left individuals and classes at the hazard of the universal struggle inaugurated by this overthrow. It hasn't devised any system to protect the rights of the weak. The entire social and economic realm, which is increasingly ravaged by misery, corruption, fraud, vice, and crime, has been ceded to anarchy and domination by the strong.

But while the social question was completely ignored, all efforts were focused on political issues. Constitutional forms and day-to-day government activities totally occupied the leading minds. In this arena they didn't stop at destroying the old administrative system and governmental constitution; they created a centralized Administration and a governmental System based on election. Both those institutions support the democratic principle.

The political order has thus been revitalized; its basis and institutions have been harmonized with the modern spirit. Equality before the law, administrative unity, and the electoral system for national representation completed, there is no longer major reform, or consequently, any great revolution to make or to fear on the political terrain. Because these achievements have given the democratic principle the high ground, and the democratic right has been established, the only issue from now on is to *regulate, develop,* and *progressively enlarge the exercise of this right,* in order to harmonize its enjoyment with developments in social progress. However, these developments must necessarily follow the principle, and are therefore no longer perhaps important, but secondary matters.

It is because the political question is now resolved in its great principles and its major proposals that it has become of secondary importance; henceforth, the economic, industrial, and social questions take the first rank. That is why the political parties are in conflict. That is why the efforts of the old spokesmen of the old parties to revive the old disputes which have been kept alive for too long are and will be futile insofar as they do not expand the scope of their reforms. That is why the political volcano, which previously spewed torrents of fire and burning lava, now, like the dead Icelandic craters, heaves up only torrents of lukewarm, fetid, mud.

§ IV.

Torpor and corruption on the political terrain

THE old politics is dying, now dead. The old spokesmen of the Press persist, through ignorance, routine, and pride, in preaching only a worn-out faith, a deceased cult: hollow formula that no longer say anything to the Nation. With the stubborn blindness of the formerly powerful, they refuse to recognize the advent of social Ideas or to invigorate the public mind with the great principles of justice, liberty, and humanity, although the realization of these principles is the task of our century. For their part, the masses, who can be stirred up only by intense ideas, can no longer interest themselves in the miserable intrigues and shabby deals of parliamentary strategy that are offered as the only nourishment for their collective noble instincts of patriotism and sociability. Disenchantment, boredom, and disgust are at their peak in this political arena, where there was still a vigorous and unified resistance during the fifteen years of the Restoration. The public mood is falling into a somnolence, helplessness, and torpor which smoothes the way for the domination of wealth and the invasion of corruption.

§ V.

Transition on the social terrain and reawakening of the public spirit

MEANWHILE, while the drying wind of egoism and skepticism sweeps the sterile devastated fields that Humanity has deserted because it no longer has any great harvests to collect there, the field of social ideas, worked quietly by toilers long obscure, is sown and covered with vegetation. It has become the meeting ground, daily more frequented and lively, of the strong minds, the ardent hearts, the new generations, of all those, in a word, who feel love of humanity throbbing in their breast and sense that the people's destiny is on the march to a glorious future.

Thus our age witnesses the extinction of a former cult, of an idea past its time that has exhausted its formula and has long since ceded its important substance. It witnesses the end—the miserable end—of a political movement that has delivered its fruits, experienced its glories and triumphs, and consumed several great generations, but whose prime mission has at least been accomplished. Yet, since Humanity won't be bogged down by corruption, or halt its onward progress, our age also witnesses the birth of a new faith, the first dawning of the universal social Idea, whose beneficial rays will revive all the exalted and religious sentiments of the human soul and will soon shine upon the most beautiful, bountiful, and holy scenes in the world.

Aspects of this magnificent renewal, this glorious renaissance of Humanity, have been foreseen or predicted with great authority by all the superior geniuses of our century, and from very different viewpoints, from de Maistre to Fourier – the supreme Genius of Humanity in modern times. In the enormous solitude of his last years on the rock of Saint-Helena, the Prometheus of our age, the last representative of the genius of war, Napoleon, meditating on the future of nations pronounced the Destiny of modern Democracy to be a federation of European nations and its inevitable result, the definitive establishment of a harmonious World Unity.

But who are de Maistre, Fourier, Napoleon and other minds of this calibre compared to those clever politicians who each evening draft newspaper articles that the country hardly reads and the great Statesmen whose demagoguery paints France as prosperous and glorious!

Nevertheless, the social ignorance of these Political old Romans hasn't prevented new ideas from developing and spreading, and if one wishes decisive evidence from the parliamentary arena itself, note this: Many deputies avow to each other that they are at *the end of their political tether* – these are their terms – and that they cannot proceed any further until they finally confront the social questions.

§ VI.

The old political parties are today *immobilist* or *retrograde*

Reason, along with factual evidence of trends in current thought, indicates that intellectual activity is moving from the old constitutional politics to the economic constitution of Labor and social Relations.

Yet there are men, newspapers, and parties stubbornly clinging to the politico-parliamentary quarrels, who have no concern for universal needs, the progress of fundamental rights or the broad interests of Humanity in our time. They are occupied with various schemes of electoral reform, changes in the censorship laws, definitions of crime, modifications of jury selection, and other paltry matters of the sacramental articles and ridiculous programs of our parliamentary cliques. Rather than welcoming and studying the social questions that are becoming more pressing each day, they thrust them aside, try to hide them, or simply avoid dealing with them. These men, newspapers and parties are today the RETROGRADE or IMMOBILIST men, newspapers and parties. Although they may throw around the fine words of *Liberty, Progress, Rights of the People, national Sovereignty,* etc., and use them to lard up all their speeches and spice up all their articles, it is the direction of the ideas that determines the character of opinions. Those of whom we speak, in spite of their fine words no longer have any vital ideas and are obstacles to genuine social progress.[iii]

With these assumptions, we will now move on to review the principal categories of the modern spirit or the broader democratic party, which in France includes the entire society.

Immobilist Democracy, or the Standpat-Conservative party.

§ VII.

The doctrinaire school or systematic immobilism

The Standpat-Conservative party has held Power in France since the July Revolution.

This party has fought for the democratic principle; it has worked to insert it into the constitution and to preserve equality before the law. Even today, it gives theoretical support to the modern democratic spirit.

Nevertheless, the new constitution is only a transition between the old aristocratic Society of rights based solely on birth and the democratic institutions of the future. However, merely by blessing the principle of equality under law, this party has gained political power and social control and has decided that the principle has accomplished its work. Liberals, after fifteen years in the Opposition, are ministers; it is unreasonable to ask for anything more.

Despite their ritual language, and their reluctance to be seen as repudiating the heritage and principles of 1789, the current Power holders leave the urgent work of the present day to the indefinite future. This theoretical concession on their part is only trickery masking their egoism.

The doctrinaire School has been the pivot of this Standpat party, formed by a faction of old liberalism's leaders, to which are joined prosperous former revolutionaries, some notables of the upper bourgeoisie and the bank, and all the wealthy dolts who always hear 1793 when Progress is mentioned. These people have found it perfectly reasonable to arm the people against the former Nobility and then to profit from the masses' victories by monopolizing all the social positions previously reserved for those privileged by birth, and they denounce as revolutionary and anarchic any idea suggesting a change in the *status quo!*

The working classes and most of the Bourgeoisie are supposed to be satisfied with having changed masters and substituted a bourgeois moneyed Aristocracy for the noble Aristocracy. Let us listen to the high priest of the doctrine. In one of those moments of ministerial leisure that occasionally occurs amidst the dissensions of the Chamber, M. Guizot wrote:

> Today, thanks to *the victory of the good cause* and to God who has given it to us, *situations and interests have changed. There is no more war between the upper and lower class, no more reason to raise the banner of the masses against the elite.* . . . Not that there isn't *much more to do, much more than the most ambitious believe,* to

improve the social and material conditions of the vast majority, Bᴜᴛ the relation between the low and the high, the
poor and the rich, *is now regulated with justice and liberality. Each has his rights, his place, his future.* (Guizot, *On
Modern Democracy*).

And in another writing (*The State of Souls*):

Is it to be dismissed, this very liberty, today the most
extensive and secure that mankind has ever known? Is it to
be scorned, this general advancement of justice and wellbeing?
Are they not recompense *appropriate* for the work and
suffering of our time? Isn't there now, after so many
mistakes, enough *to please the most exacting and to refresh
the weariest?*

Yes, thanks to the victory of the people, some positions have
changed: yours, for example, and those of your friends. But the
people, the masses' needs and interests, tell us what benefit
victory has brought them? Each, you say, has his rights, his place,
his future. What you don't want to recognize is that a close study
of the proletariat's situation reveals that each, far from having *his
rights, his place, and his future*, often doesn't even have a place
in the poorhouse.
   Which is to say that these frightful affirmations lead one to
believe that all the modern governments of France must have
been overcome by a helpless dizziness and blindness!

§ VIII.

Systematic immobilism as *provocateur*

Thus are misery, brutishness, material and intellectual depri-
vation, and political and social Serfdom of the masses bequeathed
from generation to generation! Every day a parasitic currency
speculator with a single sharp deal rakes in more gold than will
be earned in a year by a hundred thousand workers whose labor
feeds a province. Every day the large capitals, acting like engines
of war, attack the small producers and the middle classes them-

selves. Yet, confronting this revolting spectacle of inequities and economic disasters, the Corypheus of immobilism, the leader of this blind party that triumphed over the former Aristocracy only by invoking justice and the rights of all, dares to say: *that each now has his rights, his place, his future!** That the reciprocal relations of the low and the high, the poor and the rich, *are today regulated* with justice and liberality!

This is what they are saying: The people who have spilled their blood for twenty-five years on a thousand battlefields, and who have made two Revolutions to win the rights of free people, have nothing further to ask of Society and Heaven.

The masses are plunged into increasing misery by continuously falling wages; bankruptcies and commercial crises constantly unsettle the economic arena; money dominates everything, buys everything, crushes everything; and statistics on crime show figures creeping up alarmingly each year. What do these miseries matter? M. Guizot and his buddies are ministers; isn't that enough *to please the most exacting and to refresh the weariest!*

But, in truth, we might think that these egoistic, cold, politicians have assumed the task of driving the suffering people to despair, and pushing them to new Revolutions. To dare speak of justice and liberality, praise God! when inescapable misery weighs on 25 million people whose work produces nearly all the wealth of France! And, when we have noted that this magnificent state of things leaves more work for the future than our exalted leaders admit, you still say that the *status quo* is enough *to please the most exacting and to refresh the weariest!*

What is taking over here: pride, cruelty, or madness? It's a question that we don't have to resolve, but we can only admire and bless the wisdom and patience of the disinherited masses, confronted by their blind rulers' outrageous provocations.

Nevertheless, if ideas don't progress rapidly today, if the Bourgeoisie don't everywhere raise up their generous voices to protest the unholy doctrines of egoism and proclaim for the lower classes the rights to Life and to Work for which they have so dearly paid; if the people, along with the Government, must

---

*Corypheus: leader of the ancient Greek dramatic chorus. [ed.]

despair of progress, tomorrow the civil war will be reborn, and we will have nothing more to do except ready our weapons. . . .

§ IX.

Split in the Conservative party. Formation of progressive Conservative party

But, thanks to God and to the noble sentiments of the century, the School of immobilist doctrinaires is in conflict. A major favorable development is occurring in the heart of the Conservative party.

There are within it two divisions that will split further apart in the future: the progressive Conservatives, and the faction that the eminent M. de Lamartine calls "Standpat."

When the Conservative party constructed a dike against the revolutionary torrent, curbing the violence or maintaining the European Peace with all its strength, we said: "Honor to the conservative party." This party has bravely performed the first part of its task, and by its success it has rendered a service to Civilization and to Humanity.

But if we willingly concede that the Resistance was glorious and legitimate as long as Society was in convulsions, we don't hesitate to declare this Resistance illegitimate and absurd when Society has returned to a state of peace and order. Now the resistance is simply systematic and blind opposition to all applications of justice and liberty.

The number of Conservatives who share our views in this regard becomes greater every day. The split is drawn and widens more and more in the heart of the old party. The immense majority rejects the pure doctrinaire spirit, and perhaps the leader of the School himself wavers. M. Guizot, whom we have taken to task as the symbol and personification of rigid governmental tendencies, no longer has the sympathy of the Chamber. Since the period when he served as education minister, he has been supported not by his friends, but rather by the enemies of M. Thiers. In France these are all those who fear war, because of its nature and also its foolish expenditures. By virtue of this, we also accept, lacking anything better, the ministry of M. Guizot. In short, the conservative party is resigned to M. Guizot. It no longer sees him as its representative. This general repulsion for the Minister's doctrines, despite his admirable talent and personal esteem, is a welcome symptom of Parliament's progressive tendencies.

M. Thiers, the perpetual rival leader of the doctrinaire School, doesn't share Guizot's systematic antipathy to progress, but is equally undeserving of the progressive title. In history as in politics, M. Thiers believes in nothing, values nothing, and respects nothing except success. M. Thiers personifies only restless ambition and parliamentary intrigue. Profoundly skeptical in order to be ready for any sudden conversion, no opinion can count on him, and no party believes in him, unless it is a party of dupes. Therefore, we don't have to be concerned about M. Thiers in our examination of contemporary opinions, since M. Thiers doesn't represent any idea or opinion.

Thus, the Standpat School, or the systematic Resistance, doesn't have such a great number of experienced politicians as we might be tempted to believe. If we except the pigs, the ambitious placeholders, and the High Barons of the bank, there will remain only the tremulous, these good people who claim that today we would be living in the best of worlds, were it not for the dissenters, the worthless fellows, and the utopians.

The healthy part of the conservative party goes along with progressive and organizational Democracy. It is beginning to sympathize with the suffering of the masses and to welcome ideas that could result in an amelioration of the people's condition without compromising rights already attained. Men of this disposition are lacking only great passion, the sacred fire of Humanity, and the Science of progress. We must excite them and educate them.

§ X.

The split in the old conservative party's publications

The internal movement that we have noted at the heart of the conservative party is necessarily reflected in its journals.

The *Journal of Debates*, trying to keep the sympathy and the clientele of both factions, has sketched in its columns a party of vast dimensions so that each may find there some politics according to his taste. If it leaves a place on the journal's ground floor for *Defender of the poor*, it brings to the first floor an ardent apologist for financial Feudalism. The speculator, frightened by a vivid portrayal of the poor's misery or by a courageous appeal to wealthy philanthropists, is quickly reassured by reading in the column above a magnificent pleading against the People for the profit of the big bank. But if, according to the Gospel, the same slave cannot serve two masters, the result of its Janus-like politics is that disputes occur everywhere—in spite of the intelligent and truly progressive articles that it sometimes contains thanks to the healthy faction among its Editors.

The Press, more advanced, daring, and intelligent, and freer in its direction than the *Journal of Debates*, can easily stand for the paper of progressive conservatives. *The Press* condemns immobilism, and urges the Government to seize the initiative in social progress. It often reminds us that the Dynasty created by the July Revolution has a special mission to organize Democracy.

The *Press* has performed a major service for the Government by drawing a crowd of intellectuals away from the Opposition. For the benefit of the Conservative party, it has counterbalanced and mitigated the errors of the egoistic politics personified by the doctrinaire School's leader.

The *Globe*, a journal founded to sustain slavery, retains its status as the Standpat-Conservatives' *Official Monitor*. The *Globe* has bravely accepted a task that it carries out with enthusiasm, but enthusiasm isn't enough to revive a lost cause.

We haven't been concerned with those journals of the systematic opposition that gravitate around a negation or a political notable with vacant opinions, or that argue endlessly about parliamentary intrigues. These journals no longer represent any Opinions; they do nothing but stir up the dust.

If our Society continues to experience great catastrophes, we say again, these catastrophes will be the result of the immobilist Conservatives' continuation in power. If as we hope, it soon embarks on the contrary course of regulated, peaceful, Organizational Democracy, it will go there with the progressive Conservatives.[iv] Retrograde Democracy or the revolutionary party.

Retrograde, revolutionary Democracy is divided into two factions which are quite distinct, even hostile: one is *political*, the other *socialist*.

§ XI.

The purely *political* party of retrograde Democracy

The first faction consists of those considered the extreme left, and the remnants of the republican party of 1832 and 1834. It sees itself as the heir of the Convention's political doctrines, although it has lost—at least in its journals and its leaders—that celebrated Assembly's tradition of grand sentiments, and it is inspired by only its worst traditions.

Its newspaper is the *National*, a profoundly retrograde journal, hostile to social progress, enemy of any new idea, and stubbornly condemning all those who seek to emancipate the working classes by the peaceful Organization of Labor method.

The Standpat-Conservatives, without having any more love for social progress than the men of the *National*, at least permit the discussion of such questions because of their devotion to liberty. The politicians of the *National* barely tolerate these discussions, pursue them with an extreme vexation, and shamefully, sometimes even try to stir up attacks against them by a Power they detest. The leaders of this party thus show how much liberty would have been allowed to the Press, to discussion, to intellectuals, and to progressive ideas, had the bad luck of France let political power fall into their hands.

Overthrowing the current Government is the only goal of their pathetic efforts, the only idea of their politics. To overthrow the Government in order to seize Power; to set France at war with all the European monarchies; to create 45 million armed enemies on our Eastern and Northern borders by attempting to conquer the Rhineland provinces and Belgium; "to throw the most spirited and generous section of the proletariat onto the revolutionary battlefields" (Quote from the *National*); to remove all economic restraints: those are the major political points that these blind men offer for restoring the dignity and well being of the French people! Universal Suffrage, which they advocate boldly in its anarchic form of sudden, total introduction, is a revolutionary tool, the lever by which they hope to achieve their great plans.

As for their political doctrine, the philosophy of their system (if one can so speak) is the substitution of a temporary magistrate for a hereditary monarch as head of State. That is their great political and social panacea! Only if France agrees to elect its monarch every four years to be installed at the Tuileries in place of the hereditary king, a type of President named for four or five years that would be an elected and temporary office like the ex-Regent who made Spain so happy, will the era of happiness, liberty, and justice dawn! It is unbelievable that with four thousand years of history and examples of existing republican regimes under our eyes, for example, in Switzerland or throughout America, there can still be people so foolish or puerile as to base the prosperity of France on such a simple change in government structure.

This coterie without ideas or foresight that stubbornly refuses to consider the Organization of Labor, these men dead to progress, don't want to look ahead. They can't understand that war is the characteristic of barbaric times, that in humane Societies the genius of productive, abundant industry is replacing the destructive genius of conquest and revolutions, and that the regulated and equitable organization of Peace and Labor is the great issue, the supreme question of the age. This party, which has for long been leading the *Tribune* and the *National* off course, and which still includes young, generous, ardent spirits (who undoubtedly will defect sooner or later for better ideas), represents the *exclusively political* faction of revolutionary Democracy.[v]

§ XII.

Socialist party of retrograde Democracy

The second faction, the *socialist* faction of revolutionary Democracy, which is very distinct from the purely political faction, is more advanced than the latter, in that it gives priority to social reform over governmental reform.

Its leaders are intense men, bold spirits outraged by injustice and inhumanity. They have been forced into extremism by the apologists for the current order.

These men see unfolding before their eyes the spectacle of cruel and endless economic struggles, veritable civil wars where the weak must certainly perish, the masses reduced to collective servitude through the rule of money, the large capitals crushing the small, Proletarians and Paupers increasing daily, and all nations covered with a vast shroud of corruption and misery. They see the whole product of social labor flow into the coffers of the stock-jobbers, whose parasitic industry doesn't increase the nation's wealth by one centime; they hear the lucky ones, the men who possess wealth, rank and power, exclaim in the face of these iniquities: "*In a free economy rank and fortune are the signs and rewards of work and ability* (or even virtue!), *and misery will no longer oppress any but the lazy and immoral.*" This tyranny of Capital and Landed Property (which has led to such odious and revolting exploitation in Ireland that the head of the Tories has just confessed in full Parliament to *property crimes!*) has filled the socialists with noble indignation. These men consider the institution of Property itself responsible for all the plagues of the current system, and all the iniquities of our perverse economic organization. Believing that it is the eternal root of despised egoism, they repeat Rousseau's retrograde curses against the first man who, having cultivating and enclosed a field, said: "*This is mine.*" They radically deny the right to Property, defining Property as *theft*, and seek its abolition.

Rousseau was consistent in his retrograde doctrine, his negation of Property: he drove it straight to the most brutal Savagery. Logically, he also cursed the arts, sciences, and progress; he anathemized thought itself. He certainly knew that the concept of Property is a formal element of human individuality, and that it would be impossible to eliminate it without destroying that individuality, just as man would no longer be man if thinking, the supreme human attribute, ceased.

We mustn't think of abolishing Property; its development is closely bound to the development of Humanity. It has brought man from the savage state and repeatedly given him the many benefits that his magnificent genius has created in the arts, sciences, and industry. On the contrary, we must discover and embed Property in institutions that are more perfect, secure, free, mobile, and at the same time, more *social*, by harmonizing the individual and general interest in all spheres. We must create collective property, not through promiscuity and the chaotic and barbaric EGALITARIAN COMMUNITY OF GOODS, but rather by HIERARCHICAL ASSOCIATION, a *voluntary* and *intelligent combination* of all individual Properties.

The negation of the right to Property is thus a retrograde idea. It is furthermore, insofar as it negates an enormous social and human interest, a revolutionary idea. However, we must say at the outset that the men who share this negative slogan divide themselves into two very distinct camps. On one side are the English Owenites, the French Icarians, and Communitarians of various types who reject all recourse to violence and rely only on time and persuasion for the success of their doctrines: these are the *purely socialist* Communitarians. On the other side are certain Chartists and the Babeuf-inspired Communists who are determined to make a great Revolution. They argue that the community of goods can be achieved and enforced only by martial law, and that egalitarian leveling must be maintained with an iron hand. The latter are the *political* communists.

The harsh attacks directed by the Saint-Simonian School against the legitimacy of inheritance have recently reawakened and fomented these anti-property doctrines, which are spreading rapidly and quietly among Society's malcontents. Governments cannot prevent the destructiveness of these doctrines except by eliminating their causes, because they are simply extreme protests against the inhuman and odious economic regime that grinds Labor under the gigantic millstone of Capitalism. Governments and the upper classes would be wise to speedily recognize Labor's rights, so that it will make its peace with Property. The only means, the sole healthy path, is the Association of Labor with the advantages of Capital.

If the egalitarians have a defective solution to the social question, at least, as we have said, they understand its paramount importance. They also strongly reject the doctrines of the political revolutionaries. Several of their leaders have fallen out with the *National*, and have indicated that they believe its Republic and universal Suffrage, as long as the masses remain uneducated and disadvantaged, are simply procedures for exploiting the People by a small Aristocracy of bourgeois and republican dictators, and nothing more.

§ XIII.

The legitimate principles of each party

Intelligent people wouldn't join in a completely mistaken cause. Every party has a purpose and a legitimate principle. Their flaw is their exclusivity, their negation of the other principles: they are usually sound in those principles they affirm and defend.

Let us review their legitimate sides by examining the various categories of democratic opinion – the modern temper – that we have just broadly sketched.

Immobilist Democracy appears truly ignorant, blind, egoistic, and unjustified, by ignoring rights and interests seeking recognition and the requirements for progress. But it is legitimate in so far as it represents, in society and humanity, the principle of *Stability, Conservation,* and *Resistance* to *intemperate* movements towards false progress, those violent, revolutionary impulses of political or social Retrogrades.

Stability in the social realm is the first of the two conditions for the normal life of society; Progress is the second.

Order, however imperfect, and preservation of acquired rights and existing interests are elements of sociability equally important and sacred as the recognition and furtherance of new interests and rights.

When some men in Society violently attack Order or acquired rights, it is easy enough to find others pledged to the exclusive defense of these rights and to Resist all change. Usually a party that is mistaken and limited doesn't develop in a social milieu without creating, by the law of antagonism, a mistaken and limited opposite party.

The Bourgeoisie, triumphant in 1830, was liberal in principles, and basically it is still strongly attached to the general ideas of modern Democracy. It was surely not philosophically hostile to liberty and progress. It was in reaction to the violence and riots of the republicans that a single-minded violent politics of Resistance developed in its ranks. It created a strong dike against the torrent.

The pacification of republican outbursts was soon followed by the conservative party's transformation, and it is certain that if new revolutionary violence erupts, the immobilists would soon be reduced to a small number of blind men, deprived of all influence on Opinion and public interest trends.[vi]

Revolutionary Democracy, although illegitimate in its negative and subversive methods, is legitimate in its demands for the masses' political rights, which the leaders of the dominant political groups *do not even recognize in principle*, and in its support for social rights to life, liberty, and progress, *unrecognized in principle* and *denied in practice* by the grim social System that the opposition party seeks to perpetuate.

Finally, the old royalist Party, which has long resisted the democratic trend of modern Society, nevertheless represents a legitimate element that is very important in the life of Societies: that of the historic Tradition, the inherited bond between the future and the past. This party includes the descendants of the men who gave France its current boundaries, and created its independence and nationality. This party, steeped in the laudable sentiments of national pride and martial grandeur, has held in trust the eminently noble principle of Fidelity.

Therefore, at the base of each party there are legitimate human and social principles for which these parties are really the guardians. It is only because of its worthwhile aspects that a party can attract members. The good elements, the justifiable positions, alone attract and engage the majority of each opinion because men are men and not demons. People go where they see the good. They can be mistaken about the means, but they never pursue evil knowingly and for its own sake.

We mustn't then attack the deepest beliefs of each party and pit against each other the principles and interests enrolled under opposing banners.

What we must attack are the egoistic leaders and vacuous spokesmen directing and exploiting these parties, forcing them to maintain narrow, exclusive, and hostile positions in order to dominate them more easily.

In summary, each party is the guardian of a principle, a great interest, or a legitimate protest. Sincere men of all opinions must not pursue the success of their party as an entity, but that of the legitimate principle at its base.

Progressive Democracy, or the Party of Peaceful Reorganization.

§ XIV.

The good people from the old parties rally on the ground of pacific Democracy.

The present situation and state of mind is characterized above all by the general abandonment of the old political battleground and the dissolution of the former parties. Putting to one side the growing communist opinion, the quick overview that we have just given on contemporary opinion is now almost historic, as the extreme parties have rapidly weakened over the last ten years.

As we have established, the new democratic spirit was at first manifested in the political realm. Because it didn't gain mastery without challenge, its sole concern was the struggle against the antiquated pretensions of the *ancien Régime*. One might believe that the political arena was the only place where reforms were required in order for all to go well in the world. Great disillusionment was bound to follow such an expectation. The July Revolution was a definite victory, but a deceptive one. The political victory yields only so much; evil remains embedded in the entrails of Society and is steadily devouring it. In the protests and violent struggles that followed, the political terrain was still the arena. These struggles are ending.

Already, sincere, good natured, and generous men are deserting in droves from the battlefield of old quarrels; they are withdrawing from these moribund parties in which any man of worthwhile sentiments and ideas now suffocates. From the ranks of the former centrists as from those of diverse opposition parties, each day men are leaving who believe and even announce that the time for sterile discussions is past. They are saying that we must discard the old formulas, broach the economic and social issues, and work for the nation's prosperity. We must promote Association and the brotherhood of classes by regulating and organizing Work, and the Association of nations by organizing the world for Peace. Stability and Progress, Peace, Work, Organization, preservation of acquired rights, extension and legitimation of new rights; those are the formulas which are already being heard everywhere.[vii]

If the nation's activity is dying out on the political battlefield, it is reborn on the fertile and glorious field of social labor.

A nation doesn't move in one day from an old idea to a young idea, from an established creed to a new creed. Great revolutions do not occur serially except in a time of transition, indifference, skepticism, and even corruption. But Humanity comes out of these transitory crises with stronger faith, loftier hopes, and greater charity.

Therefore, from the debris of the old political parties there arises the generous and wise who break loose from the crowd, gradually dispel their mutual hostilities, and bring them into a higher sphere in order to reconcile the diverse principles for which they had been blindly fighting.

It is to these liberated men – animated by good will and noble aims – that we have the heart to speak. It is on these alluvial plains, on this well prepared fertile soil, that we must sow the seeds of the future.

These men, weary of the present scene, disapprove of immobilism and the economic doctrines guiding the development of modern Democracy. They are looking for a new faith. They are still talking only in terms of the general Democratic principles inherited from the revolutionary era, yet they see the need to replace mistaken policies with organic paths and methods. They have the heart for the task of our epoch; they don't yet have its

Science.

This state of mind is summarized in a formula today echoing from one end of France to the other: *Society cannot remain as it is; surely there is another way.*

§ XV.

Program of the progressive Democracy party – True and false Democracy

Here are the perspectives and general theories that symbolize the common beliefs of the men who are following these new paths.

To them, *true Democracy* is the full recognition of the rights and interests of everyone, and their progressive, intelligent, and effective organization. It guarantees and consolidates rights already acquired, declares the legitimacy of all unrecognized rights, and seeks the acknowledgement of interests that are still aggrieved. True Democracy is for them the regulated organization of peace and labor, the development of national prosperity, and the progressive realization of order, justice, and liberty; in short, it is the liberal and hierarchic organization of families and classes in each *Commune*, the *Communes* and Provinces in the Nation, and the Association of Nations in Humanity.

False Democracy is the revolutionary spirit; the spirit of jealousy, hate, and war; anarchic liberty; violent and covetous equality; exclusive and dominating patriotism; and fierce, chaotic, armed, and hostile independence.

They understand that true Democracy unites, organizes, relates, classifies, associates, liberates, and centuples well-being and the physical, moral, and intellectual development of all people, of all classes. They seek to combine all strengths in harmony. True Democracy is the development of the fraternal spirit in Unity.

False Democracy divides, subverts, destroys, impoverishes, and covers the earth with ruins. It incites classes against each other and people against their governments; it increases suffering to inflame the revolutionary mentality; it provokes and maintains hatred of all Social superiority; it stirs up systematic defiance, suspicion, and revolt against all Governments; and finally, it foments massive uprisings and great revolutionary wars as the only road for the salvation of nations and Humanity. False Democracy sows anarchy and reaps despotism.

Progressive and organizational peaceful Democracy, and turbulent and violent revolutionary Democracy, are the two extreme cases, the two opposite expressions of the modern spirit. One of these versions includes all that is true, pure, noble, powerful, and humane in the trends of the century; the other expresses what the modern age retains of an earlier violent and barbaric spirit. The first liberates, develops, and blossoms in the sunlight of intelligence; the second, which has been only a great fleeting passion, a social rage provoked by enormous suffering, persistent evils, and profound misery, weakens, pales, and diminishes each day, especially in its political expressions.

According to the newer, peaceful version of Democracy, the word does not mean "Government of Society by the lower classes." It means "Government and social organization *in the interest of all*, through hierarchical participation in public office holding by eligible citizens, *whose numbers increase with the level of social development.*" The people isn't a class; it is the totality; and government isn't blind and chaotic action by incompetents; it is intelligent and unitary action by the competent – whose numbers must constantly increase through social education and governmental action.

Such are the general principles, the common creed, and the accepted views of this new Opinion destined to carry the peaceful and organizational banner of progressive Democracy, unless egoism, materialism, and short-sighted governments force it, out of desperation, to take up the call of revolution and war.

If we are asked how many men in France already share this Opinion, we will answer: Count the number of those in France who now accept the principles that we have just outlined and who would sign on to them. You will see that the number is enormous.

And if we are asked why this widespread Opinion doesn't yet have a greater influence on events, we will answer: It is because it isn't yet disciplined, and it doesn't yet have widespread publicity and prominent Spokesmen. It is disseminated and appears in all the books, brochures, and writings of the Epoch's intellectuals, yet it still hasn't a loud enough voice. The old newspapers, which have been surviving on political quarrels, and which, like the old politicians, wish to forget nothing and are unable to learn anything, don't support this great intellectual development; on the contrary, they oppose and distort it. – To initiate its first daily Newspaper, we now raise our peaceful banner.

DOCTRINES OF THE JOURNAL
PEACEFUL DEMOCRACY

We have described the state of Society and indicated its needs; we have described the state of Opinion and indicated its trends. We must now inform the reader who we are and what we propose.

What we propose the reader already knows from the preceding discussion, because it was written under the inspiration of these political and economic principles. We will summarize them shortly.

Who we are, we are going to tell you frankly.

§ I.

Who we are

We toil in obscurity, inspired by a sincere love for Humanity, seeing all men as brothers, the weak and oppressed especially, but even those whom we attack most harshly for mistaken ideas or unjust power.

Most of us, from our earliest days, have had a natural tendency to explore social and political questions—those problems relevant to the fate of the suffering, who are, alas! all of Humanity. These studies have resulted in deep convictions, full of promise and bountiful hope. We have tried to share them with our fellow citizens, our peers, and our brothers, and spread these beliefs for the world's benefit, through the free and wise voice of intelligence and progressive, powerful, and authoritative experience.

We weren't writers or journalists; we became writers and journalists in order to propagate our convictions, giving up our careers without regret for a vocation that we believe is useful and holy.

At first we were regarded as innocent dreamers and utopians.

We have continued our efforts. Our first successes brought on many types of attack; we haven't been spared from accusations and unjust condemnations. We have kept going. Our convictions sustained us; the love of Humanity gave us the strength to persevere. We knew that were on the path of truth, reason, and good; we always persisted. Our first principle is that man is made for truth and goodness. We were therefore certain of gradually obtaining respect and sympathy, and winning to our views the men of good will, good nature, and honest minds – who are much more numerous than one would believe.

We weren't mistaken. We say this in the sincerity of our faith because we believe it: thanks to our devotion that Humanity will one day reward with recognition, our forces grew rather rapidly.

§ II.

Division of our Work by the increase of our forces General idea of human Destiny.

In the modern age, the great renewals in human thought and social movements are made though books and technical writings where the new idea is advanced in a scientific, philosophic, artistic, or religious discourse as appropriate; and through newspapers where the general principles are applied to those subjects and the day-to-day concerns that catch public attention. That is how the writings of philosophers, poets, and economists of the last century and the beginning of this one, together with newspapers and the speakers' platform, have worked to bring about today's successful movement in the political order.

We have followed this natural progression. We have written various works and will continue to write them and to stimulate serious works devoted to renewal, according to the great principles of the Association of Humanity, Science, Art, and Philosophy; and to develop the social reality of Christianity, by which we mean Fraternity and Unity, the supreme goals of our doctrines.

At the same time we have worked to create in the world of public opinion a platform without which our efforts would be fruitless and our ideas unknown to the public. We have founded an outstanding periodical.

Designed to popularize the Theory and Techniques of social Science, this periodical is basically a Review, explaining to educated men in mostly Scientific terms the ideas of the great Genius whose enlightened discoveries are the basis of all our efforts, CHARLES FOURIER.

We have a general scientific conception of the Destiny of Humanity. We believe that Humanity, impelled by the breath of God, is called to create an ASSOCIATION growing ever stronger, of individuals, families, classes, nations, and humankind, which form its elements.

We believe that this great Association of the human family will reach a perfect UNITY, by which we mean a Social Status where Order will occur naturally and freely from the spontaneous agreement of all the human elements.

This theoretical view presents a general conception of universal Life, which applies to the past, the present, and the future of Societies. Thus, it includes perspectives on History, on contemporary Politics,[viii] and on the ultimate Organization of Societies.

Our periodical, by its basic objective and its character as a weekly Review, treats all three of these subjects, and most especially the last.

The growth of our movement has led to a simplification of our work, by dividing duties and separating the subjects. The *Phalange*, by becoming a nearly daily newspaper, must naturally be concerned with current, practical, and Socio-economic issues, and leave to books and special brochures theoretical developments related to those ultimate social institutions that we may regard as the most perfect, but are a far cry from current institutions. Besides, only current issues can attract public attention in a frequently appearing newspaper, which presents the best opportunity for instruction and initiation of new ideas.

This progress has impressed a movement favorable to our ideas and opinions. The *Phalange* has become more and more accessible to intellectuals who don't know or don't share our ultimate doctrines. The public regards it less and less as a newspaper written by utopians and designed for initiates. People who are the most biased against us have started to appreciate it and to approve of its Politics and Socio-Economics. These are simply practical applications of our general principles of Association, Organization, and Sociability, to solve current problems. Consequently, those who appreciate these solutions recognize little by little the merit of our principles and begin to look sympathetically at the whole range of applications.

§ III.

The neutral and independent ground to which we summon all progressive thinkers

We have then, independently of our other work, developed the old *Phalange* into a ground on which all the good intellectuals, the moderately progressive thinkers, and the sincere men of different political factions, philosophies, or religious persuasions, can give us their nod, while maintaining their reservations about Theories about which they know nothing, or which they support to only a limited extent.

The more we bring everyone onto this ground, which will be the basis of *Peaceful Democracy*, the more quickly and surely will we further the great causes of human Sociability and ASSOCIATION, which is our ultimate goal.

Our task, as apostles of an idea that we believe leads to Humanity's prosperity, health, peace, future Happiness, and liberty, is to broaden this ground as much as possible to provide easy access to those of all persuasions and especially to those still critical of our dreams for the future.

Now what we hear everywhere is that the public isn't shocked or frightened by our ideas or principles, since when we apply them *to current issues using ordinary language*, they are deemed beneficial and sane. What frightens and puts people off are *technical terms*, those *formulas* that are regarded as our *scientific argot.*

Therefore, in the daily paper that we hope will reach many, and to move those now stuck in narrow partisan thinking about our broad ideas of Organization, universal Peace, and Association, we must strip away these technical terms and formulas, which have their place in specialized works, in scientific articles in the *Revue*,[ix] and even, within limits, in Miscellaneous articles in a daily paper under the rubric of a philosophic, literary, or social Study.

For that reason, in introducing the *Phalange* as a daily paper, thanks to the resources we have gained and the dedicated cooperation of many partisans who share our political and social views, we have selected a title that would seem less rarified and be more understandable by the public.

§ IV.

Reasons for changing the title of the *Phalange*

This change had its price. Under the name *Phalange* we had attained sincere respect and esteem among even those who didn't share all the journal's doctrines. We had the pleasure of seeing each year bring greater recognition, testimonials from outsiders, and disinterested praise— for its spirit of truth, justice, and absolute impartiality; for the wisdom and generosity of its politics; and for the relevance of its social research.

But the name, drawn from our own technical terminology, confused many people. Many still believed that one must be an initiate in Phalansterian studies and doctrines in order to read and understand a journal called the *Phalange*, and that reading this journal was the equivalent of endorsing Theories that were being described in ridiculous and false terms by ignorant and malevolent journalists.

The name *Phalange* was particularly suitable for a journal that was primarily concerned with the institutions and organic laws of the societary system. It could be appropriately used again by a Review devoted to the specific study of these ultimate questions, but it wasn't as suitable for what the *Phalange* had evolved into. By appearing three times a week, it was now focused on developing its principles in terms of current problems.

It mattered to the success of our principles and to enlarging the circle of readers for our daily paper, which must have the widest possible radius and bring *everyone* the message of Peace,

Association, Humanity, and the Future, that the publication not appear to anyone, even mistakenly by a narrow interpretation of its title, as the paper of a social sect, of a tiny Church enclosed in its formulas, jargon, and private rituals.

For this reason we have had to choose, for a journal that we intend for everyone, a title taken from the language of everyone, in our century's common idiom. We wished this title change to serve as a formal advertisement to the public that our newspaper is situated on a terrain accessible to those of good will and intelligence, without the need for any doctrinal preparation. All men of order and progress, friends of liberty and justice for all, will be able to join us.

Once the change was decided upon, we didn't hesitate for long over the choice of the new title.

§ V.

Reasons for choosing the title *Peaceful Democracy*

Inspired by the most incontestable principles of Christianity and philosophy, the human spirit has now started its advance, *in the name of the rights of all*, to accomplish progressively the emancipation of the weak, the suffering, and the oppressed, and the Peace and Association of peoples, in order to finally establish the reign of God and his justice, proclaimed eighteen hundred years ago by Christ.

This great movement of the modern spirit, which every day becomes more self-conscious, can be characterized by the word DEMOCRACY.

In its universality and the peaceful, generous, and organizational meaning that it has brought, especially in recent times, to the national debate, where it is embraced by all shades of opinion and in the writings of highly respected wise and progressive journalists, this word is destined to become the watchword of our epoch, the banner of the great movement regenerating modern societies. As we believe that our principles are destined to lead this movement, it is therefore we who must carry its banner.

The word *Democracy* is the most profound, universal, and

powerful word in current discourse, the only one that has a promising future in serious discussion. How mistaken it is to conceal its power because of its continued use by the revolutionary parties, in order to be respected by the most extreme conservative party speakers and journals. This observation is decisive.

The word has been and is still being interpreted by the parties in very different ways that are often mistaken and dangerous. The political and social enigma is presented to all in the same terms, but all do not know how to resolve the enigma. Thus, there appear false solutions with fatal consequences.

The more powerful the word in the minds of the masses the more it is destined to become, and the more supremely important it is for society that the masses not be led into its disastrous interpretations.

The revolutionary parties today use the word *Democracy* as a banner of revolution and war, a big stick, some against the government and political order and others against property and the foundation of social order.

We must take this weapon from their hands; we must spirit away this banner. The stick and the banner of war must be converted into a tool and flag of peace, organization, and work.

However, the attack we must make against revolutionary democracy is a purely intellectual one. God forbid that we would ever launch against any doctrines blind repression or the material weapons of Power. We must win the war of ideas. The people must judge freely between the contenders. We must demonstrate and persuade that those who are now agitating for a victory devoid of political rights are tricking and exploiting the masses, and that the true democrats are the people's true friends who don't incite them to revolt and war but teach them their social rights, demand their recognition, and pursue them peacefully through organization.

We alone today are in a position to offer this perspective and conviction to the people, because to do that, one must have an idea and sense of the people's rights and future that is superior to that of these false friends and their political opponents.

In sum, it is because we feel ourselves strong that we will vigorously seize the word *Democracy*, and strip it away from those who abuse it.

It is a bold move, and it is also a smart move, because the peaceful and organizational interpretation that we will give loudly and clearly every day to a word that inspires all the warm and generous hearts, rallies all those who truly love the people, and excites the masses will be a great service to society. The whole society will grant us recognition for this. The advocates of freedom and emancipation, youth eager for progress, and sincerely democratic spirits who don't confound Democracy with hatred will follow our banner. As for the Standpat-Conservatives, we will force them to recognize this word as it serves the general aim of social Stability or Order, which they are unable to do.[x]

Finally, in order to finish with our title, let us add that all the people can participate hierarchically in governing society once it has universalized well-being, developed all capacities, and associated all interests. The word, Democracy, even in its direct etymological sense meaning government of all by all, characterizes the Social State that is the most advanced that humanity can attain, and encompasses our broadest ideas. The most important function of Humanity when it attains its complete development in future Harmony will certainly be *self-government.*

The word suggests the issue of our time, the emancipation of the working classes, at the same time that it encompasses the broadest progress for the Future. We couldn't have found a stronger and more appropriate title for these times.

In order to complete the general exposition of the political and economic doctrines of Peaceful Democracy, we need only summarize the principles that have inspired this work. We will do this using as an outline the slogans inscribed on our journal's banner.

Fraternity and Unity

Vos omnes fratres estis,
Ut omnes unum sint

We have inscribed these two words in the highest rank, these two revelations of Christ, Fraternity and Unity, which are the alpha and omega of social Science, the base and summit of every great humane policy.

"You are all brothers, children of the same God, members of the same family." "You must become ONE single body, ONE single soul, ONE single mind, and be ONE with God." Every law, religion, and revelation of social policy and human Destiny is summarized in these words.

We have taken these words from the Gospel, because it is the Gospel that has revealed to the world the enlightenment and supreme Truths that it contains, and because we wanted to demonstrate an act of faith in these social and religious Truths that are the base and summit of Christianity itself.

Christianity is the great Religion of Humanity. Christianity can develop further, and it will certainly always continue to evolve. To believe that there will some day be a Religion for Humanity other than the one that has revealed its existence and its Unity in itself and in God is an illusion. *The individual and collective Union among men, and their individual and collective Union with God*: there will never be for mankind a more sublime principle, or a different one. Furthermore, this principle is Christian. Thus, from the scientific perspective of pure human reason we know that Christianity, which arose from the Creation, will become, with infinite developments compatible with its principle, the last Religion, and the sole universal Religion of Humanity.

Lately, people have tried to create new Religions. They believed Christianity finished, dead, and buried, and wanted to replace it so that society would not remain without Religion. The idea was well-intentioned, but it was wrong.

Christianity isn't dead, far from it. The spirit of Christianity has never been more alive, widespread, and generally characteristic of intellectuals.

The modern political and social mentality at its best is nothing but the pure spirit of Christ. Voltaire himself, when he was denouncing the evil genius of War and Massacres with such holy and relentless anger; riddling all types of oppressors, usurpers, and bullies with penetrating sarcasm; and demanding rights for Humanity with all his moral strength—what was he but one of the most powerful apostles of Christ, imbued and overcome by the very spirit of Christ that he mocked?

One has seen the old oak stripped of its rusty leaves in winter; one has seen the dried branches fall; and one has thought that the venerable oak was wounded at the heart and was dying. But the yellowed leaves fall making way for the new leaves. Each season has its flowers and its fruits. The temporary and worn outgrowths fade and die; the base is eternal. Christianity, which has broken the chains of slaves, and given women and children the first step towards liberty, has as yet completed only a first draft of its task.

Religious Unity; Free Inquiry

Religious Unity encompasses all other Unities. We believe that humanity is destined to attain all the Unities: political, social, industrial, scientific, etc. But it is clear that it will not be able to achieve religious Unity, which synthesizes all the other Unities, except insofar as those are developed and actualized.

If there is a realm that is in essence free, it is surely that of conscience. It is therefore through freedom of conscience and free inquiry that humanity must attain religious Unity.

Unenlightened blind faith, which rests only on passive obedience of the mind, isn't a religious faith; it is a coarse and brutal fetishism. Religious Truth can't contradict other Truths or Reason, which is God's Word implanted in mankind, the light enlightening every man present in the world. It is therefore by free inquiry, and philosophical and religious studies which aim to reconcile Religion with Science, that religious Unity will be attained.

Furthermore, where Unity matters the most and where it reaches its zenith is in the concept of Love for humanity and Adoration of God. It is there also that among all the truly religious men of our times Unity is actualized. Interpretation, dogmas, and the particularities of belief remain in the sphere of liberty and variety whether one observes all religions as a totality or looks at each of them individually. That is certainly true, since Catholicism, the most rigid religious communion there has ever been, leaves thousands of matters to the diverse free opinions of the faithful.

However, the Truth is one, and man is made for the Truth; he will arrive through research and inquiry at a religious Unity more and more complete and universal. Protestantism, guardian of the sacred principle of liberty; Catholicism, guardian of the sacrosanct principle of hierarchy and Unity; and Philosophy, which operates on the terrain of pure reason, are, according to our deepest conviction, destined to agree and unite one day.

PEACEFUL DEMOCRACY will devote some space to articles on these lofty questions. In the political sphere, it will resolutely uphold the principle of absolute liberty of conscience and the protection of all creeds. The current Government may be embarked, in this arena as in many others, on an illiberal and retrograde path, but fortunately, public opinion and the legislature are better disposed. This liberty has been established; we wish it to be widely and equitably guaranteed for all, and not in the manner of false liberals who seek it in order to have the right to believe in nothing. These overly permissive false liberals—in the same breath—think civil authorities should require priests to enact rituals that conflict with their ecclesiastical principles, thus putting the Sacred at the same level as public policy.

In the sphere of conscience, all must support liberty of conscience and never the use of force, even if it were legitimate force.

Social Unity; The Right to Work

Social unity will not be freely consented to and sustained by any population unless the social system meets the needs of all classes. The propertied classes sense the need to preserve order because they have everything to lose with disorder, and Society protects their right. Let us also do for the Right to Work, which is the only *Property* of the masses, what one does for the Right to Property of the elite; let us recognize it, guarantee it, protect it, and organize it. Only under this condition will there be a foundation laid for the National Unity of classes.

As for external social Unity, it must be managed through a policy of Association that sees States and Peoples as living personalities, each having its place in the sun and its right to free existence in the society of nations. In the eyes of this Policy, war is only a remnant of Barbarism, a deplorable inheritance. The increase and regularity of scientific, industrial and commercial relations among peoples; the speed and expansion in communication; and the progress of human rights and religious sensibility will insure that war will not remain much longer a feature of a civilized, learned, industrialized, and Christian Europe.

People are beginning to understand that they gain nothing from wars that spill blood all over the world, their Common FATHERLAND. The representative system is pacifist by nature; those who pay the price of war think twice before authorizing it.

Developments in industrial and commercial relations cannot entwine nations' interests, as is happening rapidly today, without putting an ever stronger damper on war. In addition, Governments today appear increasingly peace loving. In the last 25 years we have seen hundreds of problems, which in former times would have led to European conflagrations, resolved by general Conferences and by diplomatic Meetings and Conventions.

War will not be finally eliminated until the day when the Great Powers, building on the current diplomatic practice of Conferences and Congresses, institutionalize the European Concert process by making the Congress of Powers a permanent Institution, charged with establishing international law, regulating all interstate relations, managing the association of major international or intercontinental interests, and establishing procedures for all those cases which in earlier times would have provoked wars.

This sovereign institution will be the creation of the nineteenth century. It already exists de facto; now it must only be legalized. It accords with both the interests and ideas of our time.

France has the greatest interest in putting itself in the forefront of this movement, and taking the initiative in the task of organizing world Peace. This goal is the true European mission of France, that is, its foreign Policy. Its role as a social liberator has been determined by its glorious antecedents and its noble character. France should lead the movement for the emancipation of peoples and the Destiny of Humanity. France must *make* and *organize* Peace in Europe, and not simply *submit* to it. Her momentary humiliation and weakness have no other cause than the momentary abandonment of this powerful and noble Policy.

PEACEFUL DEMOCRACY will represent this valiant and glorious Policy of peace, justice, and humanity, which is highly regarded in France and in all those nations where the new spirit is developing. We hope that it will quickly replace those stupid and blundering newspapers that constantly pick a quarrel with all of Europe. Their *Chauvinism* is as destructive to the foreign interests of our Nation as the *passive and shameful* Policy that currently demeans and humiliates France. These harmful publications serve only to create or sustain our neighbors' feelings of hostility and hate against us, deriving from events of the last century that are no longer relevant, and which are the greatest reasons for our current weakness. France, with the power to do so much good for Europe, has her hands tied because of evil. If she proceeds along the peaceful and generous path of her true humanitarian Destiny she will be great and glorious among all nations. If she lets herself be led by backward thoughts and visions of conquest, or if she stagnates further into shameful inaction, she will very soon experience the fatal descent into decadence.

Peaceful Democracy,

Journal of Governments' and Peoples' Interests

We decidedly don't share the systematic prejudices expressed against Governments. We certainly don't define governments as do the Economists and Restoration-era Publicists: *"The ulcers that we must set upon to reduce as much as possible."* We don't believe that Governments are necessarily and *a priori* enemies of Peoples.

Governments make mistakes. If some elements of Society hold absurd and unjust prejudices against them, they have done much to nourish these dismal prejudices. They often err or take the wrong tack. We must monitor them and criticize them severely when they go astray. The evaluation that we have made above of the men who now have power in France clearly shows that we have no intention of shirking this duty.

However, we believe that the interests of Peoples and Governments are basically identical. Only misperception divides them. Let us take as an example the Monarch who arouses the most violent prejudices among us, the Czar of Russia. God forbid that we would endorse the policies of the Russian Autocrat! God forbid that we would advise France to conclude a close Alliance with Russia! But does anyone believe that in the entire Moscovy Empire there is any man who loves Russia more than the Czar does? Does anyone believe that there is a single person who feels more strongly representative of the Russian Mind, the Russian Nationality, and the Slavic Personality? Who is more devoted to the glory, the power, and the prosperity of this great People and to its destiny as he conceives it? We don't think so.

Is there in all of Germany a man who more completely incarnates the desire for German unity than the King of Prussia? We wouldn't think twice about it. Does anyone believe that Prince Metternich doesn't act, as he perceives it, to promote the true interests and prosperity of the people he has governed for such a long time? Finally, what man of good faith, no matter how hostile he might be, would dare to imagine that if Louis-Philippe had in his hand a foolproof method to ensure the happiness of the French people, he would do anything other than open his hand and shower on the country universal wealth, the greatest liberty, and the most perfect order? What man would dare to imagine that Louis-Philippe would keep his hand closed? Louis-Philippe is merely King today, and these days the job of King is often difficult; he knows something about that. Well! under the hypothesis that we are posing, Louis-Philippe would be not only the King of the French, he would be their Idol and God. What more solid basis is there for establishing a new dynasty than the people's adoration?

Generally, the Monarch is the man who is the most interested in the prosperity, glory, grandeur, and happiness of his kingdom. Does he therefore always know how to promote happiness? Unfortunately, no. But that is all the more reason to *enlighten* and *encourage* governments to progress rather than *overthrowing* them.

As for us, our position is not at all destructive of Governments and Kings. We are friends of the People first, and friends of governments second. That doesn't mean we must admire all that Governments do, or for that matter all that the People might do.

The Constitutional form, with a hereditary Monarch and an elective Legislature seems to us more advanced, stable, and perfect than all other forms of Government; including the republican model. But we don't insist, as does one political School, that it is impossible to have a truce or peace in Europe unless other Nations adopt our form of Government. We leave to other Nations the task of giving themselves institutions that suit them. Their independence and dignity are at stake in this matter, and Nations don't generally look kindly upon their neighbors meddling in their internal affairs.

We therefore believe that we must live in peace with Monarchies and Republics, insofar as both treat us fairly and avoid seeking quarrels with us. Absolute Monarchies fear us more than we fear them. We must ourselves curb our militant and aggressive tendencies (that, of course, wasn't meant for the current Minister), and if we wish to have our liberty and dignity respected, we must learn to have a little more respect for the liberty and dignity of others.

We have conquered Europe and Europe has conquered us; but we have been alone against all. The balance of military glory is still tilted in our favor. Let's keep it at that, and not seek to restore the Empire. We no longer have an Emperor, his motives, or his excuses. Let us now try to triumph in Europe's great intellectual, industrial and artistic campaigns. We should remain the leader of Europe, but on the constructive path of happiness, association, and liberty for the world.

It is because these are our beliefs and principles that we have subtitled PEACEFUL DEMOCRACY *journal of Governments' and Peoples' interests.*

Peaceful Democracy is Monarchical

Too much emphasis is put on governmental Reforms. That has been proven. We have had the experiments. The July Revolution put the liberal, constitutional party at the helm of the constitutional government. Did we get all that we expected? Far from it.

We have the most perfect form of government that yet exists. We stand by it, and we are right, but it is more because of its theoretical value than for its actual practical benefits. It is above all because we are weary, and rightfully so, of Reforms, Revolutions, and great political ventures, and we have learned to appraise their true worth.

We are, overall, among the great nations the one in which there is by far the greatest degree of liberty and equality. But that still applies more to our manners and spirit than to our political institutions.

Prussia, less free than France in several important aspects, is better governed by an absolute King than we are by our Ministers and Legislature. There is no nation that is making faster progress than Russia, pulled out of deepest barbarism in less than a hundred years by its Autocratic rulers. England, Europe's venerable classical model of constitutionalism and political liberty, is the nation in which the masses' situation is the sorriest. Finally, we would certainly not change our political and social status for that of the Republics of North and South America, whose inhabitants are impoverished, despite having the most fertile lands.

In view of these facts and our own experiences, it is inadvisable for intelligent men to give undue weight to political institutions.

Let us preserve what we have won; we mustn't allow a retrenchment of those liberties for which we have dearly paid. We should progressively extend them, to improve the way our institutions work, to facilitate effective national administration, and to bring about gradually the social and economic emancipation of all those who still suffer and groan in the shadow of our political trophies. But let us be very wary of reviving revolutions and wars in order to chase after deceptive institutions and adopt some republican system.

It is a huge prejudice to believe that constitutional monarchy is incompatible with the democratic principle.

A constitutional government always follows the trend of public opinion and the truly powerful in a country. England is aristocratic in reality. Its monarchical government is merely the unitary instrument of its aristocracy. Let the ideas, manners and democratic institutions of France develop more and more, and our constitutional Monarchy will be more and more the instrument of French democratic thought.

Let us therefore generate ideas and create a massive public opinion. Then our constitutional mechanism, moved by a great national impulse, will soon grind the good grain that the nation entrusts to it.

If France had been republican in principles, manners, and traditions; if it had constituted a Republic in 1830; and if the republican form were now the operational and governmental mode of France, we would be saying: "Let us preserve our republican Government, and let it serve us to govern France well." That is exactly what we are saying about the constitutional form that France now has.

Besides, not only is the Monarchy not in itself inconsistent with the democratic element. We need to remember that historically it has been under the protection of Monarchy that French democracy has increased. It was the alliance of the Commons and the Royalty against Feudalism that was the major cause of the gradual weakening and consequent final overthrow of the feudal system.

As we have seen, the new Feudalism is now weighing heavily on Royalty as well as on the Bourgeoisie and the People.

This has created a new alliance, and this time at least, victory will not be bloody and will result in the triumph of the oppressed.

Political Unity; Election

The unity of the people and its government is a lofty goal that politics must attain.

Insofar as interests are at war in Society, opinions and classes won't be able to reach agreement. It isn't the electoral system or universal suffrage that can bring accord and harmony out of the chaos. Social Unity and the Association of different classes is therefore the condition *sine qua non* of political Unity.

On the question of political rights to electoral participation in

National government there are two Schools diametrically opposed and equally mistaken.

The materialist School is led by M. Guizot and M. Thiers. The men of this school do not recognize *a priori* political rights. They don't recognize any rights other than those the law grants. Rights for them are made in the Legislature. There is for them the *pays legal* and the rest are political non-entities.*

The other School consists of the *political ideologues.* Starting from the position that the rights of citizens are *a priori* equal, whatever be their status, wealth, or capacity, the men of this School want to involve everyone, immediately and equally, in governing Society.

One denies rights and acknowledges only positive law; the other does not take situations, appropriate means, or actuality into account, and accepts no transition or limits in the exercise of rights.

We say that the two Schools are equally mistaken. This is why:

A man dies and leaves two young children. The children are the heirs, and property rights are vested upon the father's death. The recognition of *their right* is not denied, but *the enjoyment, the exercise,* of their right is denied until they reach the age when they are able to use it wisely. They are given a guardian.

This is the way that we must reason regarding the political rights of the masses. Every member of our nation is endowed at birth with universal rights, but one must allow citizens to exercise rights to govern Society only so far and as much as they attain sufficient competence and capacity to handle safely rights so important and formidable.

This doctrine doesn't disinherit the masses of their rights, as the political materialists do; it simply postpones their exercise. But, at the same time that it justifies this postponement and guardianship, it charges the guardians with an enormous responsibility. It places upon them the solemn duty of wise management of the minors' interests, and furthermore, it obliges them to make

---

Pays legal: the very limited electorate of wealthy males during the period of the July Monarchy. [ed.]

all efforts to hasten the development of the minors' capacity, and their accession to competence and the enjoyment of their rights.

Now, if the guardians administer with egoism, if their management is dishonest, if they so much as compromise through culpable recklessness, making a mockery of the rights and interests of the minors; if the minors, at the end of their tether, revolt against their guardians, throw them out, or break off with them, the guardians have only themselves to blame for the catastrophe. Revolution is always a great misfortune, but it is one that is provoked, justified, and merited. The Guardians of the people must be careful.

Because of these principles, we will not be found among the partisans of immediate, direct, universal Suffrage, but we are well-disposed to support arrangements that would introduce more intelligence and talent, and at the same time, more liberty, truth, and order, into our very defective electoral System.

Conclusion

We have concluded the exposition of PEACEFUL DEMOCRACY'S general principles, especially its perspectives on *Politics and social Economics.*

The other slogans that one reads on our masthead, those indicating our goals and objectives such as: *Social progress without revolution; Universal wealth; Attainment of order, justice, and liberty*; and those that specify our methods: *Industrial organization; Voluntary association of capital, labor, and talent*; don't require any new exposition at the end of this Manifesto. The principles that they express have been explained as much as is appropriate in an article of this nature.

The reader now knows enough about us and our doctrines to decide how far he is in agreement with them. Our Cause is the Cause of God and Humanity; our Banner is that of Justice, Peace on earth, and the Association of Nations. Let the minds and hearts set on fire by this holy Cause join with us under the Banner of liberation!

End of Manifesto

Victor Considerant's Notes to the *Manifesto*

i. Haven't new developments, since the time when these lines were written (August 1843) added discouraging proof of this great political and social infeudation to a new aristocracy in France and the other civilized nations?

ii. VC: Statistical documents collected and published recently by M. Port, head of the London Statistical Office, indicate that the standard of living of the working classes declines daily in Great Britain. These documents inform us, among other remarkable facts, that in 1824, the Smithfield market – the food market for the City of London – sold 163,000 head of cattle and more than 1,200,000 sheep, while in 1841, despite the considerable population increase since 1824, the same market sold only 166,000 head of cattle and 1,300,000 sheep. This led M. Porter to conclude that, proportionate to the population, Londoners consumed much less meat in 1841 than in 1824, nearly a quarter less.

iii. Since the first edition of this work, we happily note, there has been progress. The rights of the masses are no longer totally ignored. General corruption is coming to a head, and is completely obvious to the public. The passion for social questions has penetrated the ranks of the old politics, giving hope for a fruitful renewal of opinion.

iv. Since 1843 the conservatives, whom we hoped to see setting out on the path of progress, have shone forth, in the official arena, with only an absolute lack of ideas and character. Clearly, all the men of the current official world are incurably blind and paralytic. One can no longer expect anything now except a powerful movement of public opinion imbued with the sentiments of the French Revolution, and lighting the torch of social ideas.

v. After many evasions, the *National*, which has recently begun a frank and honorable attack on financial Feudalism, now seems to understand better the major importance of social ideas in our epoch, an importance that the *Réforme* always states clearly.

vi. However, they still lag in moving forward; the Conservatives who govern France will soon bring disasters in domestic and foreign matters to the point where they will completely legitimize the revolutionary spirit. (1847.)

vii. The deplorable and shameful direction in which the official representatives of the conservative party have taken domestic and foreign policy in recent years, by disregarding the dignity of France and the principles of the Revolution, gravely compromises these tendencies and strongly revives the struggles in the arena of power and pure politics. (1847)

viii. The word *Politics* is here meant in its general sense.

ix. We plan, once the success of our daily paper is assured, to found a *Social Science Review* that will treat the most specialized Scientific issues in greater depth than the *Phalange* has in the last three years. – This Review appeared every month since January 1845, in large octavo format, under the former title LA PHALANGE (1847).

x. The Standpat-Conservatives have persuaded us that if we have something to expect of them, it is nothing less than recognition (1847).

Index

Notes